For the Renown of His Name

Putting Christ back at the center of worship

Tim Milner

For the Renown of His Name

Putting Christ back at the Center of worship

Edited by Brad Cope and Dorilee Milner

Cover design by Kristy Reimer Photography

Contact Tim for info on booking for worship leading/ seminars/teaching

Email: tim@timmilner.com
www.myspace.com/timmilnerband
www.timmilner.com

Table of Contents

PREFACE

You have not fully worshipped God until the universe is your vision.

The Christian life for many people is summed up by acknowledging God, acknowledging our sin and choosing to obey the Lord. This is a great start; but it's as far as many Christians ever get in their walk with the Lord. Until you desire that all of creation also bows the knee to the King, your worship is incomplete. True worship means you have committed to giving the rest of your life and strength to see His Kingdom advance – in your family, your church and your world. Talk about an all-consuming passion!

In this book we'll be looking into what I've observed to be some key issues in worship that are common to many North American evangelical churches today. As I've visited and toured in over a hundred of these churches over the last decade, and spoken with pastors and worship leaders across denominations, I find common threads. (Or should I say, ropes.) It seems to me that there are foundational problems that cause many churches to fade in effectiveness as they continue to perpetuate mediocre – or even idolatrous worship. Worship is about the Renown of God's name, His fame, His eternal glory. We exist to make Jesus famous, to place His Excellency before all people. Nowhere should this be more evident than in our churches' corporate experiences of worship. Yet it seems to me that many churches have *man* at the center of worship rather than Christ.

In order to address these issues, this book will take a narrow approach to worship. I say narrow because in the Bible we discover that *all* of life is worship. Let no one say that I'm teaching that worship is only for the church service, or that the worship service is more important than private worship. A transformed life lived under the rule of God is worship's ultimate destination on this side of Heaven; the sheer enjoyment of God is the goal of worship in glory. But what happens in a *worship service* should be the overflow of what is already going on in our lives daily. As such, you'll see a close relationship between the corporate experience of worship and our own personal devotional lives.

Having said that, I've chosen to hone in on this experience of corporate worship, as we seek the renown of God's name. We'll be looking at the predominant forms that we find in most evangelical traditions in North America. We will consider how to refocus our services to help people come to the place of gaining God's vision for the universe. You will see why I consider what many churches do on Sunday mornings to not even be worship. I'm not saying it is evil; I am saying that we call much of the service worship, when in reality we actually worship only a little, or in some cases none.

I will ask a lot of questions in this book, and my prayer is not that God gives me more answers, as if what I could draw up would fit every church. Rather, my prayer is that He helps me (and you) ask better questions – questions that I hope will spawn more questions in you as you read this.

Worship leading is as imperfect an art as I am a worship leader and teacher. God is not interested in perpetuating formulas, forms and methods. Though He uses methods, the facts of church history show that whenever God's people try to capture Him, reproduce His presence, package Him and turn Him into a commodity, His Spirit withdraws His blessing. God will not be found in a *form* of worship any more than He can be confined to a *place* of worship. It is interesting to note that many people reject the new forms of worship in a move of God's Spirit today because they are holding so tightly to the forms that worked for them. But the reality is that many of the so-called "new" forms are actually a *return* to biblical expressions, not a move away from them.

This condemnation of the new is certainly a form of ignorance and perhaps even spiritual arrogance. But the similar folly is expressed whenever you find a group of people who want to throw away all the old, as if Jesus just burst onto the scene and made sense for the first time in 1995! (Or whatever other date you have in mind for the onset of true worship.) For those of you who like to complain about the old, let me ask, is it not possible that there were people fifty years ago who came to Jesus and worshipped Him with as much fervor as your generation? Were the people who gave sacrificially and built most of our church facilities any less in touch with the heart of God than you? For those of you who complain about the new, is it too hard to grasp that the young people of today are experiencing a move a God every bit as Spirit-endorsed as those you knew?

Most people want to seal the experiences and the soundtrack of worship music in a zip-lock bag and freeze them in time. Do a poll of your congregation and find that this is usually the case: people prefer the songs and worship style that was around when they first came to faith. Those experiences are the most vivid to them, and the initial glitter of their new-found faith seals them in their memory as "the way church should be." The similar parallel for most people, churched and non-churched, is that they will claim their favorite music and style as the music that was hip when they were 18-24. There is just something about that time that we just want to hold on to as the best days of our lives.

The problem with both groups of nay-sayers, young and old, is that first, they judge the spirituality of the other by their forms of worship or the absence thereof, and second, they have both lost their focus on Jesus when they stop crying out to Him and begin complaining about how some other group of people "doesn't get it."

There is only one kind of complaining that we should tolerate in church, and it's not the kind that points the finger and judges the quality of another's form of worship. It's the kind of complaining that has a finger on the spiritual temperature of a church and grieves over sin in our lives and in the body. The kind of discontent we want to see in our churches is a *holy discontent* that yearns for God's will to be done and wants desperately to see revival in worship and will not rest until all the lost are found. It's the kind of complaining that winces when Christ's supremacy is ignored in worship, the kind of unsettlement that makes people jealous for the King when they see apathy among His children. It's the kind that protests when desperation and dependence on God are pushed to the side by complacent, predictable, man-centered gatherings. I have spent most of my ministry years dealing with real-life Pharisees, who look at externals and complain about how they are not "happy" with the way things are going (often ambiguously referred to as being unhappy with the direction). Almost without exception, this complaint is a statement of preference on some method or other, or on the recent loss of forms that they found "so meaningful." This is often a spiritualized way to say that they found certain forms to be sentimentally indicative of their early years of faith and the high water mark of the emotions that were encapsulated at the time they first came to Christ.

Why do these people settle for stale manna? What God wants to give you today is more complete than what He gave you 30 years ago. He gave you what you needed to get you started in the journey, but never intended for you to think that it was utopia. Rarely do Christians concern themselves so vocally with the things that grieve and joy God's heart *now.* His desire is not to be just a memory of the past for a few to hold on to, but active in the present, to be pursued *perpetually.* And we should be ever seeking to draw near to

Him in the future, embracing every new move of God that is tested by His word.

Take this book and chew on it. Evaluate it. Some of it will not sit well with you. Some of it might come off a little brash. Some of it will resonate with you. Some of it may confront your presuppositions; some of it may rattle you. You may end up wanting to put up a picture of the author and start throwing darts at him! But hopefully much of it will encourage you and inspire you. Use what you can, discard the rest, but please, don't just carry on business as usual in worship. We are prone to laziness in worship, because to really go after the heart of God is stinking hard work. And Sunday is always coming. My hope is that you, whatever your role, from pastor to musician, to all who are children of the King, will seek the change that glorifies God and builds up your local church. I pray that God's Spirit will bring about worship renewal and revival in your church as you wrestle with reclaiming biblical, Christ honoring worship in your context.

So what are we talking about when we're talking about rethinking worship? Worship that pleases God is so ridiculously simple at its heart that some people miss it by trying to be too "intelligent." Still, it deserves explanation. Though simple, true worship is not easy, and I'm not suggesting that it is even common; in fact true worship is quite rare. But it *is* elementary, such that even a child can understand it. The almighty, sovereign God of the universe is our creator. He created all of us to bring Him pleasure by serving Him and enjoying Him forever. That's the same reason the angels worship God, because He is great. It's one of the reasons we worship Him as well, but there is so much more, something unique, a privilege and opportunity that God has given us that angels and all other creation will never understand.

Both by inheritance and choice we are vile sinners before this holy God. Because our sin separates us from a loving relationship with our creator, we were hopelessly doomed to eternal separation from Him. But God, in His infinite mercy, decided to come down to earth in person to satisfy the justice of His own wrath against us. He served our death penalty by essentially condemning each of us to death and then jumping in to die in our place.

My testimony is that Jesus paid it all for me. He's given me my life back. He's now my King and I want to live my life for Him. That's not to say I'm perfect, for I am all too well acquainted with what a rotten sinner I still am. But He's changing me continually to become more like Jesus. Instead of living for myself, He's changed my life aim to point people to Jesus and do what we were created to do, which is to revere and obey Him as our loving God. It is for our own good that He commands us to offer Him the deepest praise and devotion we have. He's a God who is serious about sin, but when we repent he turns our sorrow into rejoicing. He is a God who will never pass over a contrite heart.

And that is why I do what I do today as a worship leader and pastor. Churches are often unfortunately pegged as boring and irrelevant, and as a pastor I agree! Too many churches have either forgotten or entirely missed the point of their existence. That's why I wrote this book. Worship renwal will change everything in our churches. And I'm convinced that there are so many well-meaning Christians that have not truly entered into a worship encounter with the living God where they understand the reason we can dance and sing for Him. Every biblical option for worship is open to us. The Lord is great and greatly to be praised! (That would be as opposed to, "God is blah, and we're sitting on our hands waiting to get home to our pot roast.") Christians ought to know how to party in His presence, and it's all because of who He is and what He has done for us. Therefore, let us come with confidence before the throne of the King and never cease the wonder of telling Him how great He is and how grateful we are.

This book begins with some context on how my latest recording, *Form and Essence,* came about. Second, we'll move into laying some groundwork for developing a philosophy of worship. The final chapters of the book speak to some real world applications of worship renewal.

Chapter 1
The Album: Form and Essence

I used to dread leading worship. I was a reluctant leader all the way through college, usually getting thrown into situations because no one else was around. Don't misunderstand me; it wasn't that I thought worship leading was unimportant; I just lacked the skills and confidence to lead. But one of my most memorable "light bulb" moments happened my second year of college, when my professor went to the board and wrote out simply, FORM: ESSENCE. The discussion that followed, as he unpacked the essentials of worship and the methods of worship, has never waned in my mind. As I began to understand God's purpose in worship and the dysfunction in worship in so many churches, I became very zealous about leading. I wanted to lead people with passion and conviction.

So with that and a major revival that I was going through in my walk with the Lord at that time, facilitating worship just became second nature. About six years out of college I really had a burning desire to capture what God had been doing in my life and teaching me about worship. The album, *Form and Essence*, was to me a real marker of God's calling on my life to lead and teach worship. Now a decade plus out of College I'm writing a book about my steep learning curve in leading and teaching worship. I say steep because there really was not much available in terms of undergraduate studies in worship when I was in college. I've learned much of what I do from the good old "school of hard knocks." AKA sanctification a la whipping!

When I put the song order on this album together I really thought of it as if I were planning a worship service. There is a progression in these songs that begins with high praise and moves through the character of God and the character of the worshipper. At last it leads us to our hearts cry to leave behind this mortal body, so bound with the love of sin. Our eternal hope is to leave this fallen world, for that which is infinitely better.

In what follows here, you'll find a song-by-song description of the theology and heart behind the songs on my latest CD. This music is very much a product of my teaching ministry, and music is the medium that God has called me to use to express theology. I've included the Scriptures that I interacted with in the writing of these songs.

Bring Your Praise

© 2006 By Tim Milner

Psalm 96:8; Psalm 36:7

Verse 1

You are the holy Lamb, Almighty God
We seek Your face
We are the children of the living way
You are the Way

Pre- Chorus

And when the rain falls hard against us
We find a refuge in Your wings
And when the path You've set before us
Is hard still we will sing

Chorus

Bring your praises to the Lord
He is worthy of our praise
Bring an offering and bless His holy Name
Great is the Lord, and He is worthy of our praise

Verse 2

Your word gives power for us to live this day We need Your grace
So we walk this narrow path
But not by sight we walk by faith

Bridge

You are the Lord of all that is
We bring these praises to You now
O holy Lord, You reign in this place
Show Your power so all will bring You praise

In my years of training and ministry so far I have noticed how much better worship gatherings are (and my own personal times of worship) when we come with *intentionality* to worship. When we come to bring an offering with a listening and thankful heart, worship happens in exciting ways. That is because worship is not something done *for* us; it's something done *by* us. When we come with prepared hearts ready to dwell on the glories of Christ's name we are already in the place where the Holy Spirit can move and where the focus is sharply fixed on Christ and our walk with Him.

I was thinking about the stagnancy in one particular worship setting I was leading in. People just seemed to be rather lumpish in the pew. And one day it hit me; we are not coming to bring, we're coming to watch. Bringing is an essential element to worship. Even as I began thinking about how to bring a worship offering to God, I was inspired by what it would look like if God's people all came to bring something to Him in worship. We decided to have a worship gathering where people were encouraged to bring something to worship that was from them, directed toward God. Some brought paintings, some brought their prayer journals. Some brought their offering, others a Scripture or word of praise to share. It was a wonderful experience. The participation experienced in this event changed the way in which people approached this worship gathering from then on.

Coming to worship requires a sacrifice. The people of God have historically done this through bringing offerings, in keeping with the Bible's instructions. In fact, in the Old Testament, believers were instructed to never come before God empty handed. The sacrifices of the Lord are not just monetary, though. When I wrote this song I was thinking of an old song, "We Bring the Sacrifice of Praise." The scriptural concept is the same for both. Psalm 51 says that the sacrifices of God are a broken and contrite heart. This is the place in us from which worship and praise are drawn.

Coupled with this purpose of *bringing* praise and offerings to the Lord, is the reality that life is hard! We don't worship in a bubble and most of us regularly come into our worship times with a heart distracted over some circumstance that is just not right in our lives. The Psalmist wrote that we trust *in the shadow of the wings of God*, who fills us with the precious knowledge of His loving kindness. It is this that allows us to regularly come into His presence and bring an offering, knowing that our salvation, our earthly needs and everything else we need are met in Him.

All Hail the Power of Jesus' Name

© 2006 By Tim Milner, Edward Perronet, Oliver Holden

Phil 2:10; Isa. 45:23; Col 1:18

Verse 1

All hail the power of Jesus' name let angels prostrate fall
Bring forth the royal diadem and crown Him Lord of all
Bring forth the royal diadem and crown Him Lord of all

Chorus

And we crown You Lord of all, be exalted in this place
And we crown You Lord of all, we come to receive Your grace

Verse 2

Our Lord, our source of righteousness and savior of our souls
To Him all majesty ascribe and crown Him Lord of all
To Him all majesty ascribe and crown Him Lord of all

Verse 3

O come, that great and glorious day we at Your feet shall fall
We'll join the everlasting song and crown You Lord of all
We'll join the everlasting song and crown You Lord of all

Bridge

And we bow the knee to the God and Lord of all that is
And we give our hearts to the sovereign maker of the Earth

There is something so powerful about the name of our God. Have you ever noticed how when people curse they often incorporate the name of God? They never curse by the president or by some historical figure. Why? Because there is no real cosmic power intrinsic to earthly names. God's name is different, however, and one of the Ten Commandments talks of not taking the name of the Lord in vain.

Why is this so important? The Lord's name represents His character and His nature – His very essence. In Scripture, the name of a person is inseparable from the person themselves. When you defame someone's name you defame that very person.

The word of God teaches worshippers to love God's name. We become jealous for it; we become grieved when people use it trivially. We desire, instead, to see His name magnified. I have noticed how often people, even Christians, throw around phrases like, "O my God!" or "good Lord!" It is so rampant in our culture. Most people, even Christians, are not even conscious that they are doing it. Yet for we who love the Lord, it should not be so. The name of Jesus is the name at which, one day, every knee shall bow and every tongue confess, to the glory of God! I zealously long to see the name of my God revered. His name is holy. It is not to be made a common by-word. It is special and we, God's people, need to be proactive, even to the point of lovingly confronting a brother or sister who inappropriately, and often unknowingly, uses His name in vain. Let's guard and honor the sacred name or our beautiful Savior. I remember the first time I had to confront a brother over his use of the Lord's name. He was someone who should have known better, but had just gotten lazy in throwing God's name around. I went in to that confrontation trembling, but I just sensed that it was so important to do this. Thankfully that brother heard me and was grateful that I had gotten up the nerve to talk to him. I'd encourage each of you to think of ways to lovingly approach others about this so that God's name is revered.

The chorus of this song was written out of my desire to express the paradox of worship, wherein we come with the purpose of seeing the Lord's name exalted, and also come to receive grace from the only One who can meet our deepest needs. When a church comes to worship, it should be a time when we crown Him Lord of all and exalt Him, giving Him the rightful place of adoration. Sadly, many churches fill worship times with so many things other than worship that they miss such an opportunity.

Open the Skies

Psalm 24:7-10; Titus 2:13; Matt 24:44; I Thess. 4:16

Verse 1

We raise our shout, lift high Your name
O God to You we bring this praise.
Your love is big Your love's alive,
We stand to see You glorified

Chorus

Open the skies of heaven
And let the King of glory come in
Clothed in Your righteousness we come.

Verse 2

Proclaim His death until He comes,
Sing of our God, the three in One
Shout to declare His victory,
And hail Him as our coming King

Bridge

When You come we will be ready
When You come we will be ready
When You come we will be ready
As the Spirit testifies
As our Jesus brings us hope
'Till the Father calls the day
When the hearts of those who have followed You
Who have loved You will rejoice

One of the great word pictures in Scripture is that of Christ's return, when He rends the heavens and descends to Earth with a great shout, calling us to be forever with Him. The promise of that grand entrance is one which should fill every believer with true ecstasy and longing. I can't wait for the day when the Father calls the Son to go get His bride (p.s. that's us!) and brings us into the fullness of His glorious, eternal kingdom.

When we stand before Him, every eye will be on Him and all of the glory will be given to Him. In the mean time, the job of worshippers and worship leaders everywhere is to get us ready for that day, by living the attitudes of reverence, awe and praise that will surely overwhelm our hearts when He comes. The challenge for us is to live in such a way that we are ready. That doesn't mean sitting idly waiting for that day; it actually means being about the business of advancing God's kingdom here on earth, so that when we see Him, He will say, "well done, good and faithful servant." What judgment awaits those who live as if this life is all there is, and as if their personal kingdom is the most important thing.

I make reference to shouting twice in this song, which some may find curious. Shouting is such a wonderful biblical expression of praise and victory. I find it ironic that people at a sporting event will cheer loudly, even in front of a TV! Yet in many churches the great truths are being revealed from God's word and through the text of worship, but you can hear people coughing more loudly than you can hear them praise! You can't give a half hearted shout. It is physically impossible to shout without "giving it". It is something of the soul's expression that other forms of worship just don't convey. When we shout, our bodies join in what our soul wants to express. We come clothed in Christ's righteousness, so that when God sees us, He doesn't look at our tattered rags, but the righteousness of Christ applied to our lives, and that grace is what allows us into the Kingdom of God.

We Bow Down/ Almighty

We Bow Down By Twila Paris © 1984 Singspiration Music;

Almighty © 2006 Tim Milner

Psalm 135:6; Daniel 7

Verse 1

You are Lord of creation and Lord of my life

Lord of the land and the sea

You were Lord of the heavens before there was time

And Lord of all lords You will be

Chorus

We bow down and we worship You, Lord

We bow down and we worship You, Lord

We bow down and we worship You, Lord

And Lord of all lords You will be

Verse 2

You are King of creation and King of my life

King of the land and the sea

You were King of the heavens before there was time

And King of all Kings you will be

Chorus 2

We bow down and we crown You the King

We bow down and we crown You the King

We bow down and we crown You the King

And King of all kings You will be

Bridge

Almighty most holy worthy of praise

Creator sustainer Ancient of days

I'm not sure if Twila Paris, the original author of We Bow Down, quite had this version of the song in mind when she wrote it some 24 years ago! Easier to beg forgiveness than ask permission I guess! (Of course I got permission to use the song.)

In our English Bibles, to bow down is the most common meaning of the biblical words we have translated "worship." In the Old Testament the most common word is "Shachah," which means to prostrate oneself. The New Testament uses a variety of words that we have translated "worship", but the idea of bowing to pay homage is still prevalent. It is therefore ironic that most churches today, and most Christians at home, do not practice kneeling as they worship. Our sanctuaries are often built with no thought for such an act. No doubt this is a reaction against "pre-programmed" kneeling, which was found in most churches as an outward form in centuries gone by. The mindless expectation of the ritual soon led people to kneel without their hearts engaged. The fact that everyone was expected to kneel took away the spontaneous, devotional aspect of such an act. We really kneel on the inside, but there is just something about "proper" people in the 21st century humbling themselves by voluntarily bowing down that puts our lives in proper perspective to our Holy God.

The ideas of this song are simple, yet profound; that He is, at once, Lord of Creation and Lord of my life. The chorus says, *King of all kings You will be.* Again there is that theme of the future hope of our worship when God's kingdom is a universal reign, unlike now where we are striving for the day when His will be done on earth as it is in heaven. The apparent contradiction here is really a matter of our finite minds compared with our infinite God. Psalm 135:6 says that the Lord does whatever He pleases, yet we know that He has allowed this marvelous thing called free will among mortal beings, who often choose against God. So without opening up a great, heated (and centuries old) debate, suffice it to say that there is a *sense* in which God *is* Lord and a *sense* in which He will *yet be* Lord of this earth. I don't have the space here to elaborate on this theological concept, but it is a worthwhile study. Just don't get stuck on it and miss the big picture!

The term "Ancient of Days" is one of the names of God. When the title is used in the book of Daniel (the only place it is found in Scripture) it refers to His position as sovereign, eternal judge of the universe – something we would do well to call to mind as we worship.

What I had in mind for this song was like being in a great field by moonlight. What is in the middle is the firestorm of God, and I really wanted to convey the majestic presence of God with a sense awe and fear. The old hymn line "His chariots of wrath the deep thunder clouds form and dark is his path on the wings of the storm" comes to mind.

Step By Step/ Give You Glory

By David "Beaker" Strasser © 1991 BMG songs inc;

Give You glory © 2006 Tim Milner

Psalm 34:1; Psalm 134; Psalm 63

Verse

O God You are my God

And I will ever praise You

O God You are my God

And I will ever praise You

Chorus

I will seek You in the morning

And I will learn to walk in Your ways

And step by step You'll lead me

And I will follow You all of my days

Bridge

And I'll stand and give You glory

And I'll praise Your name forever

This has always been one of my favorite songs. Such a simple truth from Psalm 63, but what a perfect declaration of worship: "God, You are my God, and I will ever praise You!"

The idea of seeking God "early" has been taken by scholars to be literal or figurative. Some think it means early to start out the day seeking God in His word and prayer. No argument there. One time I was teaching a worship workshop and someone made an observation that it could just as easily mean that we should seek God in the "morning" of our lives; that is, to give the strength of our youth to His service. Either way, the commitment to learn and walk in God's ways is the daily prayer of a disciple eager to learn from Jesus how to live life.

The concept for the chorus is from Psalm 34 and Psalm 134; the idea of standing, blessing the Lord, and having His praise "continually on our lips" is such an important discipline for the worshipper. It is a song where the worship of our lives meets the "worship setting." Someone who comes to offer worship through this song can't just so easily leave the assembly and forget about what they have just declared. The chorus I wrote is a declaration of our intention to make His praise glorious in the presence of other worshippers in the corporate setting. This also means living a life that readily gives praise to the Lord. As I wrote it, I just felt like there was another place this song needed to go. To me this song is one of those songs that puts the worshipper in the proper frame of mind for worship in a hurry. These are words that drive home something of the seeking, following, and pressing hard after God that should always characterize the life of a worshipper.

I'll stand and give you glory... This line was written specifically at a time I was trying to find a way to teach the church I served to experience God in worship. I often encourage my people to sit or stand as they wish in a worship time, cultivating the freedom that we want to be genuine and do what is a natural response, not always having to do what everyone else is doing. It is a very powerful thing when the congregation is sitting, and then one person, without my prompting *engages* – really gets it, and is at that moment experiencing the actual presence of Christ. (This is not to deny His omnipresence, but there are special times when we actually move from believing it, to acknowledging it, and then experiencing it) Sometimes that can be a huge step of faith- to stand when everyone around you is sitting, to stand and boldly sing to your God, not caring what anyone thinks, rather seeking the smile that comes from God toward His unquenchable worshippers.

Immortal, Invisible

I Tim 1:17; Psalm 17:8; Psalm 90:11; Heb 12:29;
1 Pet. 1:15,16

Verse 1

I will hide myself in the shadow of Almighty God
I will give my heart to the One who gave me life
And though the shadows of this world all fall around me
You are my rock You are my hope
And I put my trust in You

Verse 2

I'm consumed with a passion to know You more
And what I see just draws me closer to Your flame
To honor You is what I know You gave me breath to do
In a dry and weary land where no streams of water flow
Your glory leads me on

CHORUS

You alone are holy
You alone are awesome in Your power
You are my creator
Immortal Invisible, God only Wise
Immortal invisible, God only Wise

As much as I love to remake hymns, the *Immortal, Invisible* we have in most of our hymn books was able to evade my butchering. I just had to start from scratch on this one, so there's really no evident parallel either lyrically or musically to the hymn of the same title.

I love the word picture of hiding ourselves in the shadow of His wings; it is a place of surrender – also a place of safety, as a hen gathers its chicks under its wings. It is also a place where we are shielded from the inaccessible, blazing light of His presence. I think of someday riding in the clouds with our Warrior King, sheltered under His wings, as it were, as He goes about to conquer. We will someday get to be in that place of perfect view, watching on, as our God, at last, executes justice on all His enemies.

Our God's holiness is fleshed out by the verse of the song, speaking in terms of being consumed with a passion for God that draws us to His holy flame. That holiness is the holiness we are told to reflect. He says, "be holy, for I am holy." Whenever we meet with God in worship, His holiness ought to be the first thing that strikes us about Him. He is unique; He is pure; He is *other*. He doesn't fit into the neat little categories that we would like to establish for Him. He alone is the proprietor of holiness. He is the author of life, and our response moves us to a declaration of our intent to stay close to Him through the storms of life.

He is Immortal, not like us. He is the everlasting God, invisible. He is not confined to time and space. This is the God of our worship.

If We Confess Our Sins

© 2006 Tim Milner

Psalm 32:1; I John 1:9; II Timothy 2:13; Romans 7

Verse

If we confess our sins and turn our hearts from wrong to right
He is faithful and will hear us when we call His name
You're a faithful God
Faithful when I fail You
True to Your word Your promise is sure

Bridge

When I've sinned I will call on that matchless name
Your mercy will cover me
Though I've failed You before You remember no more
I call on Your mercy again
Forgiven I'll praise You again

Chorus

Forgiven I will live to praise You
When I remember what You've done for me
From the dust of all my sin and shame I'll rise to praise You again

This is one of those songs I worked at for probably five years. I loved the verse, but I could never get the rest of it to the point where I thought it was usable. Two weeks before we went to record the CD it all came together.

The song is about forgiveness and the joy of knowing we are forgiven. Even the music walks through this crescendo of contrition, confession and finally the release of being forgiven forever to love and praise the Savior. The Psalmist wrote that it is such a blessed state to know that God forgives our sins when we ask Him. The New Testament echoes this fact; when we agree with God about our sin and ask for forgiveness, we see that He is always faithful to His promise. Because He lives in us, His faithfulness to us is tied to the fact that He cannot deny Himself and cannot lie, nor go back on His word. In short, a salvation that cannot be earned by our faithfulness cannot be lost by our unfaithfulness.

Paul wrestled with the two natures inside of him; the desire to sin and the desire to be holy. So long as we live on this earth we will always fight with that tension. When I was younger I used to beat myself up over my failures. I really thought that the more miserable I felt, the less God would punish me. I would often get myself into trouble and then try to get myself out of the mess. I thought, "since I got myself into this mess by neglecting to consult God, how could I ask Him to help me out of something He told me not to do in the first place?" How foolish I was, and am. Romans 8 begins (after Paul had wrestled with this very issue) with the profound truth that we are no longer condemned in Christ. We don't accomplish anything through morbid introspection; it just distracts us from God's grace and really praising Him for what He's done. It's not about how unfaithful I am; it's about how faithful He is. Hopeless depression over our failures is actually idolatry of self. Some people actually enjoy feeling miserable about sin, thinking that God is honored by replaying and re-experiencing the guilt and shame - as if God will not punish us if we punish ourselves. I used to believe that, but what a wake up call when I learned that this was being done at the expense of rejoicing in what Christ has done for me. When God lifts us up from the shame of sin, it is with the intent that we might rise to praise Him... again.

Incarnate

© 2006 Tim Milner

Gen 12:3; Isa. 43:10,11 ; 1 John 4:2,3; John1

Verse 1

O Come and adore Him
Come and see this thing that God has done
The lowly Child in the manger
The gift God's Son, the chosen One
A Holy God made a promise
To the children of this fallen world
Eternal life springs from the manger's Child
O let us not forget His faithfulness

Chorus

You alone bring salvation You alone never change
We bring praise for we have no gift
That could ever say enough that could ever compare
So we fall on our knees raise our hands in Your name
There's no God like Jesus
Forever Your name be praised
God Incarnate

Bridge

Purge away this idolatrous notion
That makes of You less than who You are
Our mighty warrior coming in splendor
Jesus You are the Almighty God

A holy God made a promise... That truth provided the impetus for writing this song. God, by His very nature, is incapable of breaking His promises. The incarnation of Christ and the whole Christmas story is rooted in the faithfulness of God. And that's why I often say that Christmas is supposed to be about worship -rather than most of the sentimental "seasonal music" we see happening today in churches around Christmas time. Worship is supposed to focus on God and not the objects or ambience of the holidays. The incarnation of Christ and the emptying of Christ (kenosis) are weighty and worthy theological concepts that I have tried to explain simply in this song. And there is more to unpack than I could ever fit into a four-minute song!

The deity of Christ is on display in this song. Historically, people have been known to err on the side of the deity of Christ, while rejecting or downplaying His humanity. On the flip side, there have been times when people have neglected His deity and thought of Him merely as a man. The fact is that you will blow your circuit board trying to figure this one out; you just gotta believe that He is fully God and fully man. He's not a 50/50 mix. He wasn't God on Monday, Wednesday, and Friday and then man on Tuesday, Thursday and the weekends! He didn't at some point become God, or cease to be God at any point during His time on Earth.

My concern, as a pastor, is that we display Christ fully in His deity and humanity. He eternally existed with the Father before creation, so He is not a created being. He is in no way less God than the Father and Spirit are; He is not anything less than the great I AM, the Creator of the universe. In a day when heresy abounds in pseudo-Christianity, I wanted this song to set the record straight as to what the Scriptures teach about the nature of Christ. The Word of God is very clear that we are to firmly defend these truths and purge out any trace of teaching among us that would suggest any deviation on the revealed person of Christ. *There's no God like Jesus, forever His name be praised - God incarnate.*

Of All the Things

© 2006 Tim Milner

Isa. 42:5; Isa. 40:8

Verse 1

Jesus the Joy of loving hearts
You're the fount of life You give us breath
Turning from the pleasures of this world, we run back to You
Your truth has never ever changed
In uncertain times Your word remains
The sure foundation for our lives
Lies within the truth you gave us

Pre-chorus

'Cause You came to us You came to set us free
'Cause Your love brings life abundantly

Chorus

Of all the things we know You are – You are the risen Lord
And Your name, above all names shall stand
Let all the earth send up their praise

Verse 2

Christ has for sin atonement made
I am redeemed by the price You paid
I praise You for Your cleansing blood that makes all things new
And now I'll follow in Your truth teach me to love the things You do
Breathe on this wandering heart O God
'Till thoughts of You consume me

Bridge

And there's nothing left that I can do
But to lay it all down again and follow You

This was a late addition to the album, but it is one of my favorites. I honestly just picked up the hymnbook one day and said, "I'm going to write a song from something I read today." This is not the way I usually write songs, any more than I would open the Bible, point to a passage and preach. But if you are familiar with hymns you'll see what I mean. It is kind of a hodgepodge of lines borrowed from a half dozen hymns. *What a Wonderful Saviour* is the hymn that got me kick started on this one, but there are others too.

Jesus the Joy of Loving Hearts... "What an interesting hymn title," I mused. We cannot truly be a loving heart until we have received love from Jesus. According to God's Word, He is the joy, the prize of any heart that has learned how to love. It makes perfect sense; a loving person is one who is captivated, motivated and dedicated to the Savior and the love He brings.

You can see then, that the theme of this song is greater love for the things Christ loves. The chorus is a simple and non-negotiable statement that Christ is the risen, eternal Lord and that all the earth should give Him praise. A life spent any other way is wasted.

When Morning Gilds the Skies

Psalm 5:3; I Cor. 10:31

Verse 1

When morning gilds the skies
My heart awaking cries
May Jesus Christ be praised
Alike at work and prayer to Jesus I repair
May Jesus Christ be praised

Verse 2

The night becomes as day
When from the heart we say
May Jesus Christ be praised
The powers of darkness fear when this sweet song they hear
May Jesus Christ be praised

Verse 3

You nations of mankind
In this your comfort find
May Jesus Christ be praised
Let all the earth around ring joyous with the sound
May Jesus Christ be praised

Verse 4

Be this while life is mine
My melody divine
May Jesus Christ be praised
Be this the eternal song through all the ages on
May Jesus Christ be praised

I can remember as a young teenager playing this song at my home church straight out of the hymnbook. I was twelve years old when I became our church's full-time (and only) pianist. It sounded a bit different in those days. Still, this is the only song on the album that sings in its original hymn form. If this song does have a chorus, it is in the simple repetition of the phrase, "may Jesus Christ be praised." As simplistic as that may sound, that is really all there is to life. Our lives should resound with that intent always.

In the months before our recording sessions I had toyed with whether or not this song should make the album. I was attending a leadership summit with my church, and one day, while out on a walking break, I heard the bells at an old church peel the noon hour carols. They played the hourly chime and then started playing that song. It was as if the Lord spoke to me just then, and I made up my mind that this classic hymn would be retrofitted and included on the CD.

There is something about worship in the morning that is so fitting. Of course, if you're like me, you prefer to worship corporately in the evening. That also has biblical precedent (Psalm 134). But there is nothing like waking up to a beautiful break of day and soaking in the morning sun while having your personal devotions. I'm actually not much of a morning person, but there have been seasons in my life when I was actually awake to see sunrise everyday, or was at least waking up with the sun. Conversely, I spent 3 years working shift work with my father's business and when I was on night shift, it was such a relief to see the sun come up, because that meant I could finally go home and get some sleep. Another small way to praise Jesus! To gild means *to overlay, as with gold.* So let's remember the golden goodness of God each day that He lends us breath.

On a lighter note, pertaining to morning and all-nighters; when we recorded this song I distinctly remember being in the studio working late into the night with my guitarist on the album, Kendal, and my producers. Kendal had to fly home the next day and we were nowhere near being done with all I wanted him to play on the album. At about 3:00 AM we came to this song and this cool guitar part came out. It was brilliant, but Kendal was so bushed that it took him about 20 tries to nail it. Even all the Red Bull we drank was losing effectiveness at that hour. Ah, but the morning was already coming!

Fear You Again

© 2006 Tim Milner

Psalm 103:3-7; Psalm 130; Col 1:18

Verse 1

There was a time when all we knew was Your glory
There was a time when every heart would bow in reverence
O Holy God, Consuming Fire
So pure that none could dare to look upon Your face.

Chorus

If You O Lord should mark my sins
O Lord how could I stand
But there is forgiveness within your love
That You may be feared
That You may be feared again

Verse 2

There's nothing more that I desire to be where You are
To know the fullness of Your love Your holy presence
O search my heart Consuming Fire
Remove my sin that I might look upon Your face

Bridge

We love your praise we lift Your name
We call unto You mighty God
We gaze into Your glory now
O God be praised be lifted up again

This is a re-make from the first live album I recorded in 2002. The message is one that I think churches need to hear. In my experience, I find pockets of believers who have a reverence for God that comes from a true biblical understanding of the "fear of the Lord." Some churches pride themselves on being so "New Testament" in their approach to worship, but they somehow mistakenly think that our holy God has changed, like we can approach Jesus as our "buddy-buddy," without bowing the knee to Him as master and Lord. Our way of approaching Him has indeed changed, since Christ Himself is our great High priest, but in worship we must still regard Him as holy. True worship always contains an element of awe and reverence for God's holiness. In Leviticus chapter 10, after Aaron's sons were struck down for violating God's holy commands, Moses had to remind Aaron that those who want to come near to God must first regard Him as holy.

I love Psalm 130; contained in it is one of the great mysteries of the faith. *There is forgiveness with You, that You may be feared.* I wrestled with the meaning of this well before the thought for this song came along. How does forgiveness bring about fear? Well it seems to me that the answer (as almost always in scriptural interpretation) is found in the same passage. If God were to deal with us according to our sins, none of us could stand before Him. We would all be rightly condemned to our doom. If judged fairly, my sin would result in eternal separation from a holy God. One aspect of the fear of God is to realize that He is the sovereign judge of the universe, and judgment day is coming. Until we understand how much our forgiveness cost our Savior we will never appreciate what our salvation means. We should be undone, in the same way that Isaiah cried “woe is me”, when we realize the lengths that God had to go to in the story of human history to make a way for us back to Him.

So my prayer is that through this song, the fear of God will be re-instilled into our churches. I want to see churches with such an acute awareness of God’s awesomeness, that worshipping together is an awe inspiring experience because of the sheer reverence that grips everyone.

The words in the first verse might be misunderstood by some. *There was a time when all we knew was Your glory...* In this verse I am not suggesting that there was a time when Christians were perfect, nor that there was ever a time when hypocrisy was not present in the church. But I am looking back to the church’s beginning in the book of Acts where we read phrases like, “fear gripped everyone” and “everyone kept feeling a sense of awe.” So many churches give lip service only to the ministry and person of the Holy Spirit. As a result we build churches that look and feel more like man made institutions than the body of Christ. The Proverbs say that the fear of God is the beginning of knowledge. I have done a study on the fear of God which I often teach in worship seminars. We’ll talk more about it in chapter three. It doesn’t take very long to see the kind of results that appear in the lives of disciples who have learned the fear of the Lord. The sum message of this song is a desire that the true Christ be exalted once again in our wayward churches; that people would again learn to give Him the preeminent place in worship and would dwell on His character and nature as they worship. Such a focus would stand in contrast to the consumer Christianity, the idolatry of tradition, and the social-club mentality of so many churches today.

Is Anybody Thirsty

© 2006 Tim Milner

Luke 9:23; John 7:37

Chorus

Is anybody thirsty?
Is anybody tired of living for themselves?
Is anybody thirsty?
Is anybody tired of living for themselves?

Verse

Jesus said, "If anyone would come after Me
Let him deny himself, and take up his cross and follow Me"
Jesus said "if anyone is thirsty
Let him come to Me and drink
And never thirst again"

Bridge

Take away the love of sinning
Draw us to your holy fire
We want to live our lives
for something bigger than we are
For the One who died for all

I wrote the verse for it back in the spring of 2005 for the church I was serving at the time. We were working through Rick Warren's "40 Days of Purpose" and I really wanted our people to enter the gateway to understanding our purpose in life through this song. I never really did anything with the song again until just a week before we went to the studio. That is when the chorus came to me, and it became track number twelve on the CD.

This final track should need very little explanation; it's based on the words of Jesus. I wrote this song as a call to worship or a closing to worship. This song was one of those last minute gifts from the Lord as I went to record the CD.

Each of us has an innate thirst that only Jesus can satisfy. We look so many other places, but only Jesus fills us. The call to follow Him is costly and it means denying our right to ourselves. Jesus said, "If anyone sins he is a slave to sin." Why do we sin? We sin because we love it. We love what sin offers us – but it leaves us empty. We love how it feels – but it leaves us despising our actions. We may not think we love sin; we may think we hate it, when in reality we may only hate the *consequences* of sin. To truly love Jesus is to hate sin. That is why I wrote; *take away the love of sinning,* actually an old hymn line. I hope you will wrestle, as I have, with our own broken need for the Savior to satisfy us in all the ways we've looked other places for fulfillment.

The core of being Christ's disciple is to become a lover of Him and His kingdom. So long as we first aspire to build our own kingdoms we will never be effective or satisfied in our Christian walk. Jesus said we cannot love both our treasures and His Kingdom. We must learn at all costs to live for something bigger than we are – for something that will outlast our time on this earth. And God will do this work in our life, based on His promise. For many of us, that may mean a season of God stripping away our ambitions or resources to teach us reliance on Him, and the folly of ignoring the "Kingdom among us." God took me through such a season in my first year of college, and again during my third year in a different way, through breaking my will and showing me that my empty ambitions were a thousand miles off the course He wanted. It was in these dark times that He revealed to me that the joy of a life invested in God's kingdom reaps eternal rewards, which I will never lose. Earthly investments and success of any kind, even many good and noble pursuits, are ultimately doomed for the fire. Only when the Spirit causes us to become tired of our earthly pursuits will we be ready to lay them down to take up the yoke of Christ. I was thirsty and Jesus is the water. Now I often pray before a worship time that people will be brought to the end of their proverbial ropes, because that's where the Kingdom is best entered. When all else fades, only what's lived for Christ will matter.

Chapter 2
The God of Our Worship

I grew up thinking that the most important thing in life was being good and not making people upset. My home church served up generous helpings of rules and starvation portions of grace. I've served in a few situations like that since. Thankfully I found out that the most important thing about us is really our relationship with God.

In one sense, no amount of writing will exhaust the subject of worship to an infinite God. However, in another sense it is remarkably simple. What you believe about God is the most important thing about you. What we believe about God must be affirmed through His Word. In other words, we won't discover any truth about God that His word does not already speak to. And we must not allow any part of our experience to contradict the word.

The Bible tells us that we are created for God's glory – to exalt His name – to make much of Jesus Christ and the good news contained in His word. We were made for His pleasure and not the other way around. As Rick Warren says in his book, *The Purpose Driven Life,* until we get that straight, nothing in life will make sense.

If we are to worship, we had better know the God of our worship. All our worship hangs on what we make of Christ. There are two "Gods" in this world. There is the God who is and there is the god who we think is, or think should be. We need to be very careful when representing the true and living God in worship, and we need a balanced view of how we portray our Savior in worship. Some people like to emphasize God's power, transcendence, wrath and justice, reverence for Him and holiness. Some people prefer to dwell only on His humility, love, gentleness, meekness and friendship. Both are true of God, but worship must fully declare all the attributes of God, not just those we find appealing. This of course is why the word of God is authoritative in all we declare.

What is God Like?

God has revealed Himself through His names and His attributes. It is helpful to remember that God is not compartmentalized. There is not a part of God that is holy and another part that is loving. God is a unity. Therefore this list is organized for ease of reading, but should really be listed out as: the God we worship is the unchanging-all powerful-wise-good-faithful-holy-righteous-wrathful-forgiving etc....God. You get the point. Here's just an alphabet worth of the names and attributes of God. My editor wanted me to make an alphabetical acrostic out of it, but xylophone and x-rays just don't seem to fit in the 'x' slot. Take a moment to digest this list.

a. **Unchanging** Heb. 13:8
b. **All powerful** Rev. 19:6
c. **Everywhere** Ps. 139:7-10
d. **All knowing** Jn. 21:17
e. **Holy** Ps. 22:3/ Lev. 10:3

f. **Giving** James 1:17

g. **Wise** I Tim. 1:17

h. **Loving** Rom. 5:8

i. **Wrathful** Rom. 1:18

j. **Jealous** Ex. 20:5

k. **The Lord is my banner** Ex.17:15 (YHWH Nissi)

l. **Most High God** Gen. 14:18 (El Elyon)

m. **I AM** John 8:58

n. **King of Glory** Ps. 24:7

o. **Wonderful** Isa. 9:6

p. **Counselor** Isa. 9:6

q. **Mighty God** Isa 9:6

r. **Everlasting Father** Isa 9:6

s. **Prince of Peace** Isa. 9:6

t. **Alpha and Omega** Rev. 1:8

u. **The Word** John 1:1

v. **Faithful Witness** Rev. 1:5

w. **Firstborn from the dead** Rev. 1:5

x. **God of pity** Ps. 103:13

y. **Father** Matt. 6:9

z. **Creator** Rom. 1:25

So, our worship must be based on the character and nature of God. It is our job as those who lead to make sure that He, in His revealed entirety, is central to everything in our worship time.

What is the purpose of worshipping God?

- Worship pleases God, but He does not need it.
- We were created with the need to worship (God does not need to be reminded that He is high and lifted up, but we sure do.)

Our worship is Triune: The Holy Spirit enables us to worship Christ to the glory of God the Father. (1Cor. 12:3; John 16:13, 14; Phil 2:10,11)

How do we know Christ is being exalted through the worship in our local church?

How will we know worship is taking place?

First - Recognition of God

The preeminence and focus on the exaltation of Christ is essential. We make a conscious choice to worship Christ, keeping Him first in everything, and to not be distracted by other things, or deflect the glory that only belongs to Him. The Word of God guides us in all that this entails. This is hard to measure, but it should be evident as you evaluate your services. Was there an unmistakable sense that we acknowledged God as God today?

Second - Recognition of who we are before God

This will lead to confession and the purifying (sanctification) of our hearts. Being in His presence will invariably change us as the Holy Spirit speaks to us, ministering to the brokenhearted and challenging others with the call of obedience in all areas of our lives. We must be genuine with ourselves in worship as to the state of our relationship with Him. Worship therefore requires a humble transparency. Again, as you evaluate your services, ask your people, "Are you seeing yourself as God sees you in our worship gatherings?"

***Third - Recognition of God's desire*.**

God always has a word for His children in worship. Worshipping and loving God means there will be a passion in our hearts for those things that are on God's heart. This passion causes God's heart to become part of the fabric of our being, and we begin to pray according to God's will. This includes prayer for the salvation of the lost, the pursuit of personal holiness, and a passion for the supremacy and glory of God in all things. In short, the result of worship, when applied to our lives, is transformation, a.k.a., *change...*

John Piper puts it this way: "We exist to spread a passion for the supremacy of God in all things for the joy of all peoples, through Jesus Christ."

Our worship uses the whole Bible.

It is a mistake to write off the Old Testament as a secondary document. It is the first document of our faith, and I sometimes prefer to call it the first testament. We need to ask ourselves, what was really done away with at the cross that would cause us to not refer to the Old Testament for our practice of worship today? Is God different? Is there any less of an obligation on our part to make His praise glorious? To obey Him? To pass on the testimony of God's works to the next generation in the assembly? What was done away with then? The sacrificial system, the ceremonial law, and the elite priesthood. What changes in the New Testament is that Christ was the once-and-for-all sacrifice – so there is no more priesthood because we are all priests, and we all (Jews and Gentiles) can have direct access to God through our great High Priest. That is what has been done away with from the Old Testament. But the character and nature of God, His summoning us to worship, the content of our worship, and the sinner's response to His mercy is the same. The need to come humbly before God and the transformed character of the worshipper is the same in both Testaments. (With the bonus that we know who Christ is – and know the rest of His story!) This affects our worship deeply. As we use the whole Bible, we see Christ in the Old Testament passages too. Everything before Christ points forward to Him; every thing since Christ points back to Him and ahead to what will be. Helping people make the connection in worship is an important part of helping people read their Bibles from the perspective of God's story.

We need an ever-expanding view of God

Do you feel like you are getting too comfortable with your knowledge of God? Do you have God-in-a-box-syndrome? If you are a pastor or leader of worship and you have ceased to be fascinated with God, maybe you need to get off the platform for a season to get to know Him afresh. The angels have been with God since the beginning of time and they never cease to be fascinated with God. When pastors and leaders lose the awe of God they start to promote answers rather than relationship. God becomes predictable, controllable and domesticated. That's not the God of the Bible! For some of us the problem is really that we're over-churched, but have had so few real worship encounters - despite the thousands of hours of pew sitting we've logged! And our people will be uncommitted heel draggers (instead of committed followers of Christ) and will live purposeless lives, always groping for something more fulfilling, if that is the kind of God we continue to put before them in worship. (i.e., Yawn…Pass the beer nuts.) As a pastor I don't have enough reason to get out of bed and leave my family in the morning to give my life to anything less than an unrelenting pursuit of a pure and holy God who is active and at work today. No man-made institution is that important. The sacrifices of ministry are not worth it if we are merely going to play church. But to seek His face; to get serious about the barrier of sin; to live for a God who blows me away with His steadfast love; to foster an excitement and a passion for His eternal glory and reign; to have my heart set on nothing less than seeing more people turn to Him and live the abundant and eternal life that Jesus offers… – now that's more like it! (Phew! Pass the energy drink please!)

Here are some demonstrations of how worshipping God for who He is will change us as we truly *adore* Him, and turn the worship service back to His agenda.

Worship God in His Wisdom – When we worship God as wise, we find it much easier to submit to His commands and His discipline because we know He sees the bigger picture. If we don't worship God as wise, we're likely to think our ways are higher. This will lead to problems in surrender in worship if we suspect that there is any sphere at all where our wisdom exceeds His. The young man who is being tempted to have sex before marriage will learn to take God at His word that it's wiser to wait. The person who has been treated unfairly at work will learn that vengeance is God's department and will trust His wisdom to refrain from retaliation. How can you worship God as wise?

Worship God in His Beauty – When we worship God as beautiful, we will see how His perfect character is so desirable and so good to behold. If we don't worship God as beautiful, we're likely to see his character as flawed and even harsh. We will question the things that God calls beautiful, forgetting that He sees the inmost part. When we consider how we were made to enjoy beauty, we catch just a glimpse of the joy that awaits us when we see the Beautiful One revealed.

Worship God in His Holiness – When we worship God in His holiness, we put Him in His rightful place as sovereign and perfect, and we place ourselves in the rightful place of humility and reverence. If we don't worship God as holy, we are likely to think that God is to be measured by *our* standards. And a God that is measured by our standards is not God at all. That kind of thinking is just plain stupid. My worship changed when I began to dwell on His holiness in every encounter with Him. He is "other." He is not like me. He is sinless perfection. I need to focus on my holy God.

Worship God in His Goodness – When we understand that God is good, we interpret even our bad circumstances as being part of what is God working out for good as He defines it. If we don't worship God as good, we are likely to question whether what He does is really good because we will be working off of our definition of good, not His. God's good is holistic and eternal. And since we think in compartments and in terms of this life, we must have faith to believe that the "goodest" thing that God could ever allow is for us to become like Christ. We all know Romans 8:28, but usually ignore verse 29 which teaches us that God's good is always measured in terms of us being transformed and made like Christ. God will use any circumstance to bring that about, and will challenge the way we cling to the things of this earth to get our attention.

When I was 21 I was afflicted with a severe back ailment. As I wrestled with God on my bed for five months, I cried out like Job. (And read that book about five times!) But at some point during that journey I got it: If God was to be more glorified by me being stuck in bed than to heal me, then that was His good plan, and I would choose to glorify Him in it. Ten years later I now see His good purpose in bringing me through that experience. As a pastor I now know how to express compassion for the sick. Before my ailment I might have passed a sick person by, not knowing how to relate. Now I enjoy visiting people in the hospital, or encouraging those who are experiencing physical suffering.

And so, looking back I can think of a number of other times in my life when I questioned God's goodness, only to see that He was working out a far greater good than my immediate comfort.

Worship God in His Majesty – When we worship God in His majesty, the attraction of earthly majesty fades away and we are left in awe of Him. If we don't worship God in His majesty, we are likely to think that the things on this earth are truly glorious. We look to technology and cyber-relationships to impress us, thus ignoring or downplaying God's splendor, and giving glory to the creature rather than the creator.

There are lots of things on earth that can "wow" us, but if that "wow factor" is not leading us closer the heart of God, it is misplaced wonder. I love my motorcycle. I love making music. I love concerts. I love sports. I love my wife and my kids. But I've learned that all of these pale in comparison to knowing my majestic King. In the case of my family I learn about my relationship with God through them, but He ultimately gives and takes away. I'm learning to hold everything loosely because the things of this world are so unworthy to be compared with the majesty of my King. The paradox is that when I let go of my grip on the things I love the most, the Lord actually helps me love and enjoy my family more deeply, not less.

Worship God in His Justice – When we love our God of justice, we grasp the biblical perspective that God is incapable of doing anything unjust. His nature is just, all He does is just, and since He cannot lie, the standard of justice will never change. When we fail to worship Him as just, we begin to think that we know where and how justice should fall, and we can even become upset at God when He fails to execute justice to our liking, or executes justice in a way we don't like.

If you're like me, you would love to be in charge of lightning – just for one day – so you could mete out some serious justice on the earth. But God will avenge. Coming to terms with this in worship leaves us confident in God's justice and takes the pressure off of us to punish all the evildoers in the world. Their time is coming.

Worship God in His Mercy – When we truly worship God for His mercy we understand how unworthy we are of it. When that happens, we stop being judgmental of others who need God's mercy as much as we do. If we neglect to worship God as merciful, we become legalistic, callous and miserable. God delights in mercy and wants us to love it too. (Micah 6:8)

Maybe you feel like me sometimes here; as much as I love God's mercy on me, I want justice for everybody else! But when I see God as merciful, I repent of this callous attitude and learn to love His mercy for all who will bow the knee and call on His mercy.

Worship God in His Power – Our confidence in life comes from worshipping an all-powerful God. He is mighty to save us, to defeat evil and to help us through difficult circumstances. The daily peace this kind of worship brings us is our reward from God. When we fail to worship God in His power, we see our circumstances prevailing over us and we try to fix everything ourselves rather than praying to God, leaning on Him. If we are not worshipping an Almighty God, we are worshipping something other than God.

When I was thirteen I really wanted a dirt bike. I would go around saying to myself, "If God was really all powerful, He'd just have someone come drop one off for me tomorrow." I'd pray to that effect, and the next day there would be no motorbike, and therefore in my mind God was not powerful. I hope I've grown up a bit from there, but maybe there are still times when in more "mature" ways I still question God's power. Worship helps me to see that His power is available, not for my wish list, but for His Kingdom and glory.

Worship God in His Knowledge – When we worship God as all-knowing, we learn that all knowledge comes from Him. This helps us understand that the smartest person, even the collective brilliance of all humanity, is just steam from a kettle compared to His billows of understanding. When we fail to worship Him in His Omniscience we may think that God is not privy to certain important details in our lives that need His attention, thus we spend our time telling Him again and again what He already knows. In the worst case, we elevate human reasoning and knowledge above what God has revealed.

When I was in college I really wanted to buy a truck. I was cool. (And my neck was what color? I mean, what college student needs a truck? Chicks dig it, I guess?) My grandfather didn't think so. He said a truck would drive me to the poor house in gas and repairs. He was right. At 65 years of age he had knowledge that I lacked at 20 years of age. Just like that, God knows why some of my prayers have been left for so long. He knows what would happen to me if He granted them, so He doesn't. And so I worship the God whose knowledge far exceeds my own and keeps me out of so many kinds of trouble.

Worship God in His Wrath – When we understand God's wrath, we appreciate how much Jesus suffered in our place because of our sin. Without recognizing God's wrath we will feel apathetic about not only God's hatred of sin, but toward what our salvation cost Him. We don't understand from what we've been saved if we don't acknowledge that God will mete out punishment against all who reject Him. A view of a God who does not punish rebellion is not only inconsistent with

Scripture; it lessens the seriousness of sin, and our need for the cross.

I grew up with parents who knew how to run a tight ship. Rebellion was not an option, and I'm so thankful now. The seriousness of sin was taught in my home and I know that human wrath is pretty tame compared with God's.

Worship God as Faithful – If we worship God as faithful, we have such security in knowing that He will be true to His promises. Such trust is a cure for anxiety. When we ignore His faithfulness in worship, we end up living in fear of the future. We end up casting doubt on His promises and thus we end up putting our trust in futile objects of hope, which are not faithful at all. In so many situations in life I need to worship my faithful God. When I lost my job, when I resigned from a ministry position, when I was dealing with debt and not enough income, I've learned God's faithfulness. When I was chronically ill, when brothers in Christ have betrayed me, when friends have broken promises, I've learned that only God is faithful.

Worship God as the LORD – Worshipping Christ as the Master of our lives puts us in the proper perspective in our purpose on earth. We exist to serve, love and obey Him. When we don't exalt His Lordship in worship, we begin to think that He exists to meet our demands. We will also go soft on His commandments because we will never submit to the authority of Jesus when we don't first call Him LORD.

I lived a lot of my life glad to call Him Savior, but not ready to follow the course He had for my life. Through severing a relationship with a girlfriend (who gladly is now my wife), He brought me to that point of surrender. And as with tears I accepted His breaking of my will, I felt a surreal healing come over me as I let go of my grip of the wheel. I knew that I was doing a lousy job of running my life. I needed a new lord. I needed *the* Lord.

Worship the Lord as Creator and Sustainer– It is truly humbling to realize that we are the creature and He is the Creator. It puts all of life into perspective. The intricacies of all we see point us to the designer, and we are in awe. We must attribute the beauty of all that we enjoy to the hand of God, not chance. When we fail to worship Him as Creator, we are easily impressed by man's accomplishments, including our own. It is the Creator who gives us breath and sustains us.

When I was in my late teens, I used to be so self-assured in my ability to work a "real man's" workweek to earn the dough. Now I realize that every breath comes from Him, and that every day I go to work and come home I have none but Jesus to thank for the food on my table and the strength and faculty to both go to work and enjoy my food.

Worship the Lord as Jealous – That God is concerned about His glory and is alone declared worthy of worship should inspire us. It is for our good that he commands this. When we see that nothing in this life will satisfy but Him, and when we see that He is the ultimate worth in the universe, we will also become jealous for Him. It then becomes the worshippers' desire that every knee would bow in love and obedience. When we downplay His jealousy, we slight the words He Himself spoke that He will not give His glory to another or share it with another.

I struggled in my first year of college with this God who demanded such exclusive allegiance and would tolerate no other passions or desires ahead of Him. I thought Jesus was an ogre, when He commanded us to take up our cross and to love Him more than our earthly families. How could I love Him more than even the woman I wanted to marry? But through that same breaking process I mentioned above, I came to know that any other passion that is not first subject to Christ is misplaced. I know that my love for my wife and children is greater, not diminished by loving God in first place, above all.

Worship God as Patient – We certainly need to thank God for being patient with us, but also with others. His patience is not partial and when we understand this patience, we see our own need to be patient. When we ignore the patience of God, we can become critical and condescending toward others who need God's patience too. Understanding that God is patient should also help us be patient in the times when He asks us to wait on Him. Of course, God doesn't just wave a wand over us to make us patient; He puts us in circumstances that will make us develop it. In my case He gave me kids!

When I was about ten I used to love to make models. Model cars, airplanes, whatever. The problem was I wanted to get it together in one sitting. I wanted it to look like something recognizable right away. So I'd take the wings and start attaching stuff to them, since they were the part that was most impressive. Needless to say, that plane never got finished. I had to send it to F-16 heaven early. Even as an adult I still lack patience in many ways, especially when it comes to people. So God placed me in ministry.

But God can wait us out. If we don't learn patience this week, He'll put something in our path next week, next month and next year. He's pretty good at patiently out-waiting us. Time is not pressing on Him.

Worship God as Unchanging – Worshipping God as unchanging gives our entire faith a foundation. God is not fickle; He is not arbitrary; He is the same yesterday, today and forever. His love never changes. His blood will always be enough for our forgiveness, and our names are eternally written in the book of life. When we entertain thoughts of God changing or becoming unstable, our whole life is shaken. We may forget that His promises are sure. We may be tempted to find some earthly thing to put our trust in, which *seems* to be stable, when only God never changes. It is impossible for God to change. Change is always for the better or the worse – or a compromise in some way. (As if He could become better in a certain aspect but become deficient in another). Both are impossible for God. He can't get any better, and wouldn't become any worse. There is nothing in Him that needs to be tweaked or brought into balance. His name is I AM, not I AM BECOMING, or I WILL BE SOMEDAY… I'm humbled when I think that the same God who called Abraham and David and John the Baptist and Paul to His service is the same God who has called me to proclaim His unchanging truth.

Worship God as….?

Now you try it. Find an attribute of God and ponder what happens in our hearts when we adore God for this. Then think about the folly of neglecting this. In what ways have you experienced each of these in your own life? How have you responded to a God who is faithful, merciful, all-knowing etc…? You might even want to try this exercise in a small group or when teaching worship in your church.

Chapter 3
The Fear of God

The fear of the Lord is a fascinating study. Proverbs says that the fear of the Lord is at once the beginning of *wisdom* and the beginning of *knowledge.*

The fear of God is not just about respect. I get tired of hearing preachers say that the fear of God doesn't mean we need to be afraid of God. Maybe I don't need to be afraid of their wimpy version of God, but I will have a significant dread of the true God of the universe. Let's see, it is like falling into a marshmallow-covered pillow to fall into the hands of the living God… What? (Scripture please!) More like, *it is a fearful thing to fall into the hands of the living God.* (Hebrews 10:31) It is not until we express that appropriate fear that He summons us forth and offers us restored relationship with Him and even friendship. Realize that because of Christ, we don't fear in exactly the same way as an Old Testament Jew. However the Old Testament gives us the context to understand just what the fear of God is and how Jesus offers us friendship and not just fear. Let's consider a few Scriptures on *fostering the fear.*

Ex. 20:18-20 NIV

When the people saw the thunder and lightning and heard the trumpet and saw the mountain in smoke, they trembled with fear. They stayed at a distance and said to Moses, "Speak to us yourself and we will listen. But do not have God speak to us or we will die." Moses said to the people, "Do not be afraid. God has come to test you, so that the fear of God will be with you to keep you from sinning."

It was as if the people were saying, "Moses, you go and have a relationship with God and tell us what to do." They were afraid that if God were to speak they would die, which they would have – but the reality is that they were a stiff-necked people who did not desire God's presence. They were afraid because they knew that they were a rebellious people. God desires relationships with everyone. At this time it seemed that Moses stood alone in wanting a God encounter. God is to be feared, but that fear ought to draw us to His salvation rather than push us away into His wrath. If we try to stand off and keep God at a distance it is because of sin. If we confess our sins, we are able to have fellowship with God.

We see here that the fear of God was to keep Israel from sin. We know that they often neglected to fear the Lord and were characteristically unfaithful. We are supposed to have a conscience that tells us that there are consequences for disobedience – the most significant of those being broken fellowship with God. If we sear our consciences by perpetual unrepentant sin, we will grow so numb to the Spirit's prompting that we won't even miss the fellowship.

Deut. 6:2, 13; Psalm 128:1-4 NIV

...so that you, your children and their children after them may fear the LORD your God as long as you live by keeping all His decrees and commands that I give you, and so that you may enjoy long life... Fear the LORD your God, serve Him only and take your oaths in His name... Blessed are all who fear the LORD, who walk in His ways. You will eat the fruit of your labor; blessings and prosperity will be yours. Your wife will be like a fruitful vine within your house; your sons will be like olive shoots around your table. Thus is the man blessed who fears the LORD.

The Hebrew concept of God's desire to prosper one's family is one we would do well to imitate. We shouldn't misunderstand this as some kind of health and wealth mentality, such that only good things happen to God's people. Still there is a strong connection between chasing after God and the blessings that come from allowing His reign into our family situations. This ultimately leads to a blessed legacy and posterity for those who are to come. Children are a blessing from God; our families are a gracious trust from Him.

Deut. 10:12, 20 NIV

And now, O Israel, what does the LORD your God ask of you but to fear the LORD your God, to walk in all His ways, to love him, to serve the LORD your God with all your heart and with all your soul... Fear the LORD your God and serve Him. Hold fast to him and take your oaths in His name.

Notice that there is always a tie between service and worship. We worship what we serve; we serve what we worship. The tie is so tight between the Hebrew word for worship and our English equivalents that translators practically must flip a coin at times to decide whether to put *worship* or *serve* in our English translations. Whenever Israel went astray, it was usually with the rebuke, "stop *worshipping and serving* the gods; *worship and serve* God alone."

Ps. 19:9 NIV

The fear of the LORD is pure, enduring forever. The ordinances of the LORD are sure and altogether righteous.

This verse says the fear of God is holy and eternal. There is a unique (other) kind of fear that we have for God that we do not express toward any created thing. Fearing God is not a fad; it is not an experiment. Perhaps the fear is said to be eternal because the fear of the Lord is the kind of fear that leads to eternal life. That's not likely what a Jew in BC 700 would have thought reading this, but we can see it looking back through the cross. For sure, the fear of the Lord means loving His ways and inviting Him to search our hearts, receiving His cleansing and letting Him correct our thinking.

Ps. 25:14; Ps. 61:5 NIV

The LORD confides in those who fear Him; He makes his covenant known to them... For you have heard my vows, O God; you have given me the heritage of those who fear your name.

I love the thought of the Lord sharing His secrets with those who fear and love Him - that He actually reserves friendship for those who fear Him, and shares with them the secrets of His covenant. Seeing the full picture, we understand the outcome of His covenant to be eternal life. He has an inheritance reserved for all those who fear Him and He loves to share that hope with His children. It's that Revelation 3:20 picture of sitting across the table from the Lord as He shares his heart with us and we with Him. Check out Ephesians chapter one for more about that inheritance.

Ps. 33:8 NIV

Let all the earth fear the LORD; let all the people of the world revere Him.

Simple and to the point, the psalmist understood the Lord's desire that all of creation would universally fear and be in awe of God. We're not the only part of creation that should fear the Lord; we're just the only part stupid enough to not do it - except for the fallen angels – but they don't count; they are as good as toast! God has a plan, which will not be thwarted;

it is to draw all nations to Himself. He wants to pour out blessing upon those who will call upon the name of the Lord.

Ps. 103:13 NIV

As a father has compassion on his children, so the LORD has compassion on those who fear Him.

The fear of the Lord is a condition of His compassion. I picture approaching an abused dog, and the way he cowers. If you've ever known a dog that's been mistreated you know the look of being hunched down, ears low, tail between his legs, looking up as if to plea for mercy. I've been around such animals, and to draw near to an animal that is in such dread of you is really quite sad. He watches nervously as I reach my hand out to him. Then he realizes that I don't intend to hit him, I just want to pet him. He instantly relaxes and realizes that I'm a friend, soaking up all the affection. But it was his initial cowered position that actually drew me to him. If he had been barking angrily, defensively, I would have passed him by. Who in their right mind sticks their hand out to pet a defiant, angry German shepherd? So it seems to be with God. We have had other master's who have beat us, but God is a gentle master. If we stand off, barking, wary, He won't draw near. (Of course the analogy breaks down because God isn't afraid of people who bark.) But when we are in fear of Him, it is then that He draws near and shows us His gentleness. Just like a mistreated dog can learn to trust a new owner, so we learn that the fear of God actually draws His favor.

Proverbs. 1:7 NIV

The fear of the LORD is the beginning of knowledge, but fools despise wisdom and discipline.

The fear of the Lord is the beginning of knowledge. It seems to me that any knowledge about anything will only result in a puffing up of ones self - unless we first realize that God not only created all the things we have knowledge of, but gave us the faculties to be inquisitive and even begin to understand how He put everything together.

Proverbs. 8:13 NIV

To fear the LORD is to hate evil; I hate pride and arrogance, evil behavior and perverse speech.

The fear of the Lord causes us to hate evil. The hatred He has for evil should become burned on our hearts as we spend time with Him. In doing this work in our heart, the Holy Spirit cures us of any sense of independence of God. We see how desperately we need Him, and it is the fear of God that drives us to Him, scared as we may be.

Proverbs. 9:10 (See also I Tim 1:17) NIV

The fear of the LORD is the beginning of wisdom, and knowledge of the Holy One is understanding... Now to the

King eternal, immortal, invisible, the only God, be honor and glory for ever and ever. Amen.

God is immortal, invisible, the only wise God. He is the standard of wisdom. We will think God's ways foolish until we truly fear Him, and then we begin to see that God's ways are so astonishingly higher than our ways that we have nothing to do but worship Him in the fullness of His wisdom. The fear of the Lord is what changes our perspective. It should teach us to default to His wisdom rather than our own.

Proverbs. 14:26 NIV

He who fears the LORD has a secure fortress, and for His children it will be a refuge.

When you have your hope so firmly fixed on your Savior, you can have that strong confidence this verse talks about because you know who your Abba is. You are excited about knowing Him more; you are passionate for the glory of His great name. This is not arrogance since it is not based on you, but Him. You are excited about the life changing power of His word, you want to see people saved, and you are serious about sin in your own life and in the body of Christ. You can't be silent when things are wrong in the body, when you see people ignore truth, when the church is not going forth victorious, when the worship is lethargic. You end up on the cutting edge of vision and biblical change – for His glory's sake – not your own. Yet you can be sure that people will try to cut you down out of jealousy, their own pride, etc... It is then that we, His passionate followers, must run to that place of refuge where we will always be accepted. This is not self-sufficient conceit; it is a calm resolve to carry out what God asked us to do, knowing fully that He has called us to do it. When we have such confidence, we will not be dissuaded by people who try to stop us from doing God's will. I have claimed this passage many times in ministry when people misunderstood me or falsely accused me of seeking my own agenda in worship renewal. I know what God said, and I won't doubt it in the dark times.

Jeremiah 5:22 NIV

"Should you not fear me?" declares the LORD. "Should you not tremble in my presence? I made the sand a boundary for the sea, an everlasting barrier it cannot cross. The waves may roll, but they cannot prevail; they may roar, but they cannot cross it."

This verse emphasizes the folly in not fearing God – the folly of not seeing our smallness. God made us to rule. In fact, Jesus referred to us as gods (small 'g' of course). (John 10:34) He didn't mean that we were to be worshipped; He meant that we have the capacity to order and to reign. God has so created people in His own image, that in our sinful distortion we can actually believe that we can talk down to God. This is delusion, obviously, and God paints a mental picture for us similar to the drunk man who defiantly stands in the path of a freight train. It's preposterous to think that we could ever contend with God. And so God reminds us that we *will* learn the fear of our Great God, either on this side of eternity or after it's too late to be saved. "Who will not fear me?" asks the Lord.

Acts 2:43; 9:31; 19:17 NIV

Everyone was filled with awe, and many wonders and miraculous signs were done by the apostles... Then the church throughout Judea, Galilee and Samaria enjoyed a time of peace. It was strengthened; and encouraged by the Holy Spirit, it grew in numbers, living in the fear of the Lord... When this became known to the Jews and Greeks living in Ephesus, they were all seized with fear, and the name of the Lord Jesus was held in high honor.

Here we see that the fear of God brings the comfort of the Holy Spirit and growth to His church. How I love being in situations where we sense that fear has gripped every heart, and every heart is tuned to what God is saying. This is so precious - so rare. It stands in contrast to being in situations where every heart seems to be tuned to the things in church that are not being done their way. The fear of the Lord in Acts is not a paralyzing fear; it is a mobilizing, exciting fear that causes us to rejoice and experience the joy in serving Jesus, desirous to love and serve Him.

Philippians 2:12,13 NIV

Therefore, my dear friends, as you have always obeyed—not only in my presence, but now much more in my absence—continue to work out your salvation with fear and trembling, for it is God who works in you to will and to act according to His good purpose.

As we grow in the faith, there must always be the sense of “wow, we’re saved.” Fearing God as a Christian looks different than the Old Testament sense, because we are in direct relationship with God. As we apply this sense of high regard, reverence and submission to the ways of Christ, we find that we more consistently live out His will for us. This is the goal of worship - to live every aspect of our life under the reign of God, trembling, yet with thanksgiving and joy. What a glorious paradox is this Christian life.

Rev. 15:4 NIV

Who will not fear you, O Lord, and bring glory to your name? For you alone are holy. All nations will come and worship before you, for your righteous acts have been revealed.

The sheer magnitude of God and the magnetism of God’s glory brings fear to all creation in the final chapter of history. What dread awaits those who have rejected God and will have their evil deeds exposed before the world. And what joy for those who love His appearing, knowing that our sins are underneath the blood of Jesus, never again to see the light of day.

Evidently, God wants us to have an educated fear of Him. I remember when I was about ten years old going on a helicopter ride. I was terrified – but excited. When that chopper is spinning and making such noise, it feels like it's about 5 inches from your head. You duck and make sure there is extra, extra distance between you and it. But that fear didn't stop me from going for the ride. It was awesome! But... if I didn't have proper fear going in and ran toward the chopper, throwing my hands up in excitement without being wise to the danger, it could have been messy!

Better to foster a biblical fear of the Lord in our lives and in our times of corporate worship... What should that look like in your church?

Chapter 4
What Do We Mean By "The Presence Of God" In Worship?

Any savvy theological watchdog will read this brief chapter with ears pointed forward, and eyes focused ready to strike on any hint of error. As sure as the concept of the presence of God is misunderstood and abused by some, it is misunderstood and all but ignored by others. Let me try to explain at least three realms of the presence of God.

First, He is omnipresent. He is everywhere in the totality of His being at all times. He fills Heaven and Earth; there is nowhere we can go that He is not. These are the simple facts. We don't just turn on a switch, or play a chord, and "whoosh," we're in the presence of God. The eyes of the Lord are in every place, seeing the good and the evil. He is in Heaven; He is in Hell. If you think about it, He is omnipresent in both the worship service of His saints, and in the evil occult meeting.

The second way to understand the presence of God has more to do with us acknowledging the first truth. I like to think of it in terms of, *God is here and we are in His presence, whether we like it or not.* But the reality is that God has so made us so that we can choose whether to accept this or not. Some people live their whole lives suppressing this truth. (Romans1) But even the demons know the truth about God, and so this second truth is not sufficient by itself. Our understanding of the presence of God is not complete until we have experienced the manifest presence of God

This third understanding of the presence of God is where God changes lives, and far from it being a feeling, it is rather an actuality that also causes us to feel. The manifest presence of God is not just about feeling though. It has much more to do our surrender to the Holy Spirit. This is seen in our salvation initially and then in the daily journey toward God. You don't have to be in church to experience God this way. God loves to meet with His children. He is a God of relationship. In Revelation 3:20, He is seen to be the God who pursues relationship with us.

It is that third realm of the presence of God that we want to be concerned about in our corporate worship times. The presence of God is what causes a sense of anticipation in worship. I often pray with my team as we lead, "Lord would you fill people with great expectation for You." What drudgery it is to be in services where people come with the expectation that nothing different will happen today. We'll sing, we'll hear a message and be home in time for kick-off at 1PM. Big deal. When we foster an expectation that God is going to show up (a figure of speech, as we know He's already there), people engage readily. People are looking for a reason to engage. Many church services give us reason to disengage.

So, we could sing radio top-40 songs when we get together in the sanctuary or use the worship space for a dart competition. We could play table tennis in our pajamas. The presence of God would be there, sure. But what we want is to see people connect with the truth that God *is* present. When we let our head knowledge of that fact give way to the heart knowledge that He inhabits the praise of His people, our response should be one of, "come, Holy Spirit." It is not that the Holy Spirit is not here already, it is that we now consciously and corporately *welcome Him.* God doesn't force us into relationship; we have to accept His invitation and in a sense, RSVP His call. That is what we mean by the presence of God. It is a wonderful, powerful place when we as His children set aside a time to focus on Him. It is for want of that kind of focus that many worship gatherings never get to the place of doing anything remotely on track with worship. It could be said that God *inhabits* the praises of His people, whereas some people and their programs can *inhibit* the praises of His people.

Consider what God could do with a group of people who have availed their hearts to Him. What if the purpose of worship was to hear from God? What if the prize in worship was repentance, forgiveness and God's call on your life? What if we came to worship expecting to encounter Him? Is there a reason why people generally look forward to getting out of the worship service more than they do coming into church? Is the prospect of that pot-roast in the oven, picking up the kids from nursery, or going out for lunch really that much more tantalizing than coming to worship? Or is it that the worship is so *not* worth looking forward to, that these other things seem really delightful? The presence of God changes all that.

But be alert! When the expectation of worship is established to intentionally engage in the presence of God, you will see a measurable response in terms of the way people react (negatively) or respond (positively). Realize that many times change in worship is coupled with other changes in a church, and that people will often express displeasure in other areas of the church by taking it out on the worship service.

What happens when we prize the presence of God? Maybe people will complain, giving will go down, and people will leave your church because the services are too God focused, and not man focused. You'll never hear someone say something so audacious as that, but goats and tares and Pharisees can be very manipulative in their complaints. In fact, that is something we need to address. How often do the complaints of those who are not mindful of the things of God sway the decisions we make in terms of how we do church? (Or stated negatively, how often do these people stop the implementations we should make because of all their squealing?) Always be on watch for the telltale superficial nature of these complaints. When you hear all complaint and no praise from a certain group of people, you're probably in a situation of spiritual non-health. Remember earlier I talked about the kind of holy discontent that is from God that is actually healthy and edifying, rather than discontent that is selfish, negative and focused on surface things. *But…* you should take notice when you see people upset who *are* actively serving, giving and praying and still praise the good stuff they see, but are expressing concerns. They probably are correctly discerning that something is amiss.

I've been in situations where supposedly godly members of a church would threaten the leadership with leaving or diverting their giving. I once served in a church where one couple openly said they were so upset that they were giving their entire tithe to missions and not to the church until things changed to their liking. One couple even threatened to sue me for emotional harassment because I was ruining their church. It's hard as a pastor not to laugh out loud at these "take my ball and go home" tactics. They reveal pretty significant spiritual immaturity and a lack of understanding of the nature of the church. These are the kind of people in need of admonishment and confrontation. We are not to reward this kind of dysfunction in the Lord's church.

And so, unhappy people will pick on something like volume, or the "disrespectful" style of dress of those on the platform, or the "irreverent" new music, or the service running too long, or the announcements being moved to the beginning of the service, before worship. They will make snide comments about some sacred piece of furniture on stage being out of its normal position. They might complain that you didn't properly honor the veterans on patriotic holidays, or sing a certain thematic song on Mother's Day or Independence Day. They will personally slander the character of the pastor that is perceived to have caused their unhappiness. You should know by this stage of the book that these are battles worth fighting, because people can seem like lovely saints until they are made unhappy. Then the true colors come out. Actually rather than bringing out the worst in people, change usually reveals what is already there – a shallow, "me" centered faith.

Now I've gotten myself on a little bunny trail, but this is exactly the kind of thing a church will go through when it neglects the supremacy of the presence of God. These are especially evident if you're in a church with substantial history. Some churches allow people to dedicate items in memory, which often become stumbling blocks to the next generation. Let me illustrate. "My aunt Olive dedicated that chair fifty eight years ago, and over my dead body will you move it." You fill in the item here; whether a painting, or stained glass, or a plaque, or a carillon tower, or any other item dedicated in memory. You must not allow any family's sentimentality to put a choke-hold on what God would have your church do to grow and be more effective. Stuff is just that, stuff. It's all going to burn, and in the mean time, it is made to serve us, not the other way around. I was once a pastor of a church and had a cranky old trustee yell at me to get my foot off the pew (in front of a group of about 30 people who had to witness this awkward moment). Some of you are in churches where you know exactly what I'm talking about. Don't tell me idolatry is only something Israel fell into, when some of our churches are riddled with gods and idols that people hold to be more important than making faith accessible to the next generation. Few if any churches that fall into these traps are living out the great commission effectively. Worship is not about perpetuating stale, inflexible tradition. Where are the disciples of Jesus amidst a church busy making idols of institutions and buildings? Jesus said it is better that a millstone be hung around your neck and you be thrown into the sea, than to cause one young in the faith to stumble. Of course, if we are realistic, we realize that it is not always the young who are young in the faith. There are many people who have attended church all their lives who have yet to see that they are called to serve and reach the next generation. Sometimes leadership must pull these people aside and lovingly exhort them and instruct them positively in how they can leave a legacy of eternal worth, instead of a legacy of perpetual belly-aching over such ridiculous things. Squelching future moves of God by holding on to anything other than Christ and His Word is folly.

The presence of God is exclusive. Not that we exclude *people*, but that our intentional center of attention in worship necessarily means there are other things that we *don't* do in our times of worship. Sometimes a church meeting in a neutral facility is the best cure for these problems. Buildings are fine, but a church is often more focused on the heart of being the church before it has a building. I've seen many churches first hand that start off so hungry for God and dependent on the Spirit – until they have a building. Then the turf wars begin.

So, on the other hand, if you make all these changes we've talked about, in pursuit of the presence of God, people might actually come! You may see attendance blossom, as your church becomes known for vibrant, Christ centered worship. People may leave other churches for *the right reasons* to come to a church that values and understands the purpose and focus of worship. The presence of God is what separated Israel from all the nations. It was an exclusive privilege. Now it is open to everyone, and people intuitively know that there are some churches that welcome the presence of God, and some that are far more interested in perpetuating their social club religion. The presence of God is that place from where we want to live our lives. The power and the peace that we draw from having spent time in the holy place gives us a picture of the kind of people we know Jesus wants us to be. And when we are in His presence we want what Jesus wants.

Finally, when we talk about the presence of God let's ask ourselves, who ultimately benefits from worship that is offered in His presence? I would suggest to you that it is actually us! Yes, worship is for God and directed to Him, without a question. But since He doesn't need it, He is not more God and no more satisfied in Himself as God with or without it. We are the ones who benefit from the presence of God. We are the ones who need our perspectives changed; we are the ones who need to surrender. We are the ones who need to train our minds to remember Him. That's not to say that God doesn't enjoy worship. He surely delights to hear the heart's cry of His children. He's told us as much. But He's not pacing heaven's floor wringing His hands saying, "I wish my people would praise Me. I'm feeling a little down today and I just need to hear that they love me". So it's not that we come to worship and say, "Okay everybody, let's worship poor old God. He's not getting enough of it these days, and we want Him to bless us, right?" The presence of God is *His* gift to His children. Beautifully, as we come to worship, He is glorified and we reap the benefits of knowing Him. What a gracious God we have, that He would bless mere mortals with Himself! He is the treasure. Now we understand that God's commands to praise Him are actually the most profoundly loving thing that God could tell us to do.

So let us ask:

- Does your church practice the presence of God?

- How could a focus on the presence of God change your church?

- Would people complain about so many trivial things if they lived for the glory of God, and sought His kingdom first like He told us to?

Chapter 5
The Art of Leading Worship

When I think about worship leading I like to look at it as objectively and biblically as I can. But the reality is that you and I are shaped by our cultures and our upbringing. We can't be perfectly objective because out opinions and preferences are formed based on subjective elements. Still it is helpful to ask, what needs to be common in Christ's churches around the world? What are the non-negotiables? Once we've asked these questions, then we get into the specific question: What does this mean in my church's context?

As you think about this, you will find that worship services are a lot more about how the whole church functions than you may realize.

So, it is vital that every church answer the questions about your local context, and at other times it is helpful to step back and say, "What is the priority of the church everywhere?" I get all kinds of good answers when I ask this in workshops. What is the priority of the Church? Missions, reaching the lost, worship, discipleship, tending to the poor; these are all good answers. But the correct answer is easier. *Christ* is the priority of the Church! The church is from Him and for Him and made possible through Him. Jesus is supreme to the church.

Let's remember that God seeks *worshippers*, not worship. (John 4)

Let's remember that Worship is about *our* relationship with God - I John 4:20,21; Matt 6:14; I John 1:9

Since this is the case, a worship leader must realize that the worship gathering is about bringing people from wherever they are into that place of fellowship with Him. We have 167 other hours a week to meet with one another. Can we not set aside an hour to be together for the exclusive purpose of seeking God as His church? I throw that out as a challenge. Try spending one hour sometime as a body focusing on Jesus and His word. You will probably discover that there is much misused time on Sunday morning that goes into things other than true worship.

Worship leaders need to understand that people generally are not ready to worship at a "worship service." Too much sin, distraction and disappointment in the week have left them burdened and weak. So then, we as worship leaders must help them prepare their hearts. So, very simply, there are a few places to start that really draw people in. First, the Bible places a premium on thankful hearts. (Ps 100 is a great focus.) Second, people need to recognize afresh what it is to come before their holy God, and so the confession of sins is another way to help people understand the spiritual focus of our worship gatherings. (1 John 1:9; Psalm 51:16,17)

Worship leading means "stair-stepping" a worship experience toward personal intimacy in the corporate setting. We may start off distant and distracted, but the hope is that by the end of our time together, we will be re-connected with God and re-focused on what's really important. Plan every service with this objective.

Don't let music become a crutch. It too easily becomes a default substitute for true worship. That doesn't undermine the importance of music and singing. They are biblical and important, but music needs to be engaging, not just a routine. So ask yourself, "What would we do for worship if we were in a persecuted country?" If you sing as a body there you'll be found out and that would spell big trouble. So do they not worship? Of course they do, but obviously singing is not all there is to worship. We'll cover this in detail in the next chapter.

A worship leader is a people reader

As I've said, people are not always ready to worship; sometimes leading means learning to "read a crowd." If there seems to be a resistant or apathetic spirit, sometimes the best thing you can do is address that. Break away from what you planned, and call people to prayer. Sometimes people need to be exhorted and reminded of the purpose of worship, and of the great opportunity that is theirs to meet with God in a powerful way in the assembly.

I've had times when I've dropped songs or whole parts of sets, or just started leading with only my guitar into some well known songs without the band. The bands I've worked with understand. They don't get angry that they practiced but didn't get to play. They're there to serve. And so, don't be so into running a finely tuned program that your are choke-holed into doing it, even if it's the wrong thing for a moment. What if there has just been something unforeseeable that happened that morning that calls for a change of focus? Sometimes I've led a time of spontaneous sentence prayers from the people, and some heavy themes of brokenness in people's lives start coming out. I had planned to use this time to jump into a fast song, but the mood is all the sudden more reflective. I had planned to do Chris Tomlin's "Forever," but instead opted for a more reflective song called "Faithful One," by Brian Doerksen. Both songs hone in on the same thing, but one was much more appropriate for the way God was leading His people at that moment.

Similarly, a pattern of revelation and response in worship just makes sense. Sometimes people aren't engaging because we've not given them content and context – something to respond to. I often prefer to lead worship after the sermon. If your message is pointing people to respond to God, what better opportunity to take the head truths and make them heart truths.

So now we ask, what is the job of a worship leader/worship team/musician?

Play and plan skillfully. (Ps. 33:2,3; 1 Cor. 15)

There are so many variables from sound, video, lights, and projection. It all is for the King. Let's remember that as we train people and include them in the spiritual preparation as well. Have you done everything in your power to ensure a smooth run? Check out Nehemiah 4:14. We know that without God's spirit, nothing will happen, but once we have sought Him, we are to give ourselves fully to the task. For Nehemiah that meant, remember the Lord – then fight!

Here's a brief checklist:

- Have you removed obstacles from walking paths? (I.e. cords, stands, amps etc...)
- Is the sound system set up, mixed and EQ'd properly? (With a competent operator?)
- Is your projection system working? (We hate hearing, "but it was working Thursday night!") Do you have a competent operator? Are your slides free of typig erers ?!!)
- Does your tech know where *you* are going with the songs? It's one thing to expect a tech to follow you, but experience has shown it is better let them know ahead of time as best as you know how things will go. All of us have been at the mercy of a projection operator who got "lost." Do yourself and the congregation a favor and put the slides in the right order.
- Similarly, does the pastor or others taking part know when to step up to the platform? If you're not into writing it down, develop a discreet signal system.
- Are the instruments tuned? Do your stringed instrument players have a spare guitar and

cable in case they break a string or run into trouble?

- Are your leaders working to develop stage presence? We're not talking about showmanship, but the ability to take people with them in worship. We'll cover this later as well.

Leaders, you must prepare your team for leading worship by spending time in prayer together asking for the Holy Spirit's purposes to be accomplished, namely the surrender of lives and the glorification of Christ. John the Baptist gave us a great quote that every worship leader should memorize. "He must increase, I must decrease." Stay out of the way, draw attention to Christ – not ourselves. (John 3:30) To do this you must have a servant heart – it's not about you. Take care to present yourselves as God's mouthpiece. You need to be living a life of integrity! - People are watching you on and off the platform. Are you fit for the platform? Should you really be up there asking people to do things in their hearts that you are not doing? Do you ask people to give the tithe when you don't? Have you asked people to extend forgiveness when you won't? Have you invited people to foster a passion for God alone, when you have other passions ahead of Him?

Other considerations need to be put out here as well for worship leaders and teams, which perhaps would be better termed, *worship servants.* Let's talk about such things as modesty. Please understand, we should be allowed to have casual, approachable dress on the platform; we just have to use discernment and remember that we are accountable to God and to our brothers and sisters. We really want to be serving up there and that often means putting aside our comforts and even fashion preferences so we can serve the greater good. Think in these terms: The question is not, "Can I get away with wearing this?" The question is, "Will this outfit help people not notice I'm there so they can see Jesus?" If you have a lady in your ministry who says, "Well, men shouldn't be looking anyway," then clearly, this individual lacks the maturity and servitude necessary to even begin worship ministry.

I like to lead worship in jeans and a t-shirt, but there are times when I will dress up a bit more when I'm guest-leading in a more conservative situation. It's not a matter of "can I," it's a matter of, "will this edify or distract people." Of course the flip side to this is that when I'm working in my home church situation, I'm in the role of helping people learn grace and tolerance. I had a young man in my church once who came to the Lord out of horrific circumstances and upbringing. He had a love for the Lord and great musical ability. The way he dressed on Sundays was offensive to some because it was different than the way a typical middle class white man would dress. They judged his heart by the clothes and hairstyle he had. This became a significant teaching point in the last church I served. We were trying to teach our people to stop being so judgmental about externals and look to the heart. This young man led several people to the Lord and counseled many in their walk with God. When the complaints about his attire came to me, I had to ask them, “When is the last time *you* led someone to the Lord?” “When is the last time *you* sought out people who were different than you, or even new to the church to say ‘hi’ and let them know that you’re glad they came to church today?” For some, the immediate sorrow they felt for this sinful attitude was evident. For others, this pierced their pride and they got angry. But just a few years later, I’m happy to say that this same church now embraces that young man and even made him a youth intern. That’s what we want to see on the whole in worship: unity, not uniformity.

What about flow?

As a worship leader you need to establish flow, promote God awareness and make sure people know this is not a performance. You need to weed out what is not worship. For example, why do some people feel that presenting a Boy Scout medal is a worthwhile activity for a worship service? Why do we let people ruin worship time with announcements square in the middle of people trying to focus on God? Are there not other times that we can do these things? We take such a casual, common approach to the presence of our King that we sometimes overlook Him. I compare it to trying to have an important conversation with someone who keeps interrupting you to answer their cell phone. It’s just plain rude.

One of the things a worship leader does is grant permission and let people know what's ok. Let people know that *you know* they don't know a new song; give people permission to engage or to not engage. We can't force worship, and inasmuch as we so want to see people free to express themselves, I often tell my people, "Feel free to do none of that." This actually has a freeing effect on everyone. (Phew, it's ok if I don't raise my hands!) To expect everyone to do these things is no different than old traditions that expected everyone to kneel at the appointed times. That's just replacing one form of legalism for another. (Booo! to that kind of stuff!) Having said that, when introducing something like keeling it is actually helpful to invite everyone to try it together. After that, you can give the kind of permission that says, "Please feel free to kneel, if that is what is in your heart to do today." And yet at times, as you lead and even coach people in worship, you may still find it appropriate to ask everyone to stand etc... We're not trying to make a hard, fast rule here; just a principle.

Worship leaders are to pursue godly character and transformation in the worship time, not sentimentality or some emotional experience.

How many of you have been to a worship event or conference that was a high point and your best worship experience? As great an idea as it might seem, it is very fake to try to re-create that in your service. Worship is never about manipulation. Using good ideas, yes; trying to re-create a moment, no.

Still, we may legitimately ask, *Why isn't our home church experience like the worship events I've been to?* This is an intensely practical question. I've asked this question of people in my workshops. They usually agree with these thoughts:

- We don't come with prepared hearts; we rush into God's presence, or have not been worshipping through the week.
- We are distracted with our stuff and things to do, people to organize, trying to keep track of family on the way to worship.
- We don't pray that God be glorified (His renown) in our worship. We should be praying for these spiritual aspects, but often if we pray at all, we only pray for technical things, like a smooth run etc...
- We have many other activities and focuses at the worship service than "Worship".
- We have people leading the service/ singing who don't know how to lead worship. (Worship leading is a combination of spiritual gifts + training + talent)
- We have issues/ grudges, un-confessed sin with people around us that hinder our prayers, and thus our worship and communion. (I John 4:20,21; Matt 6:14,15)
- We expect to get something rather than to give (you often *will* get something at a conference because it's bigger and better than what you know)

- People at special worship events often come bringing expectation/ intentionality. Many times we come to church bringing only apathy with us.
- We plan haphazardly or half-heartedly. *It's just church music...*
- Our artistry is mediocre or worse, or we try to use art as a substitute for heart. Just because most churches have a "praise and worship" band, does that mean we have to try to make it happen here, even if it stinks?
- Too structured/too mindful of the clock
- We compare ourselves to other churches and get caught up in hyper-criticism.

Worship leading is not for the faint of heart. Having been a preacher and a worship leader I find it's much easier to preach than lead worship. The preparation time and working with a team can make leading worship incredibly stressful. It is a lot of work and can be frustrating, even exasperating. I believe it is a calling that combines musical skill with certain spiritual gifts of shepherding, wisdom, prophecy and probably others. Just as you have heard many preachers that are boring, ineffective communicators, there are also many worship leaders and teams which lack the training and skill necessary to be convincing. Churches need to realize the value of a good worship leader. If you have one, give thanks! And if people have told you that you are one, be humbled by the notion that God would speak His truth through you. Be sure you return all the glory to Jesus.

Worship leading is privilege. In spite of the difficulties we encounter, there is something so powerful and fulfilling in helping your brothers and sisters in Christ engage with Him.

Chapter 6
Tools for Worship

I grew up in a church whose worship service you could carbon copy week after week: Song, greet, two songs, announcements, offering, song, message, song. That's it. The formula of success! I've been surprised by how many churches still practice this format, or one like it. This is not necessarily a bad thing, but there are many more things we could incorporate to make a more meaningful time of worship.

We're talking here about using the many forms of worship that we find in the Scripture. It is always helpful to remember that they are tools and options, not the measure of spirituality. Whenever introducing new forms we need to do so with the grace that doesn't make people feel that they must do this or that to be worshipping. It is good to teach on these as you introduce them. It's one thing to ask people to raise their hands in worship, it is quite another to give them the biblical context and a reason to do so.

With many of these forms you will need to connect the dots for your people so they see that these expressions can physically help them express the spiritual realities in their heart. I was speaking to a lady recently who jokingly told me, "You'll just have to be patient with me; I'm a recovering Baptist!" Well, no matter your past or present affiliation, there are many churches where these forms will seem new, even though the Scripture references will tell you that they are older that any denomination or tradition.

Some of these forms are perhaps best practiced in private worship, but I don't want to categorize them. Try them all in private and you will feel much more natural about using them in the congregation. I love to kneel before my God, but there was a time when I didn't do that even in my private worship. Incorporating it and practicing it privately now means that I can do it publicly and it's so natural I don't have to give it a second thought.

Raising hands (Ps. 28:2; Ps. 119:48; 1 Tim. 2:8; Ps. 134:2)

This is one of the most beautiful ways to physically engage in worship. What are some thoughts that would cause us to do this? Let's start with surrender. You can't fight someone if you've got your hands in the air. We can raise our hands in giving, thinking about bringing praise and giving thanks to the Lord. We can lift our hands to receive from our God a special touch in times of need. We can receive and thank Him for the many gifts he gives us. We can also receive His sovereignty into our lives in the bad times. My little girl, Kierra, loves to run up to me and hold her hands up. Without saying a word, I know she wants to be held. What an awesome picture of how our God wants us to be with Him. He longs to hold His children, so let's raise our hands!

Kneeling (Ps. 95:6; Eph. 3:14; Phil. 2:10)

The primary meaning of the word worship in the Old Testament is to kneel; it is also one of main meanings in the New Testament. Yet most churches in North America today do not practice kneeling in worship. There is something about coming to God on our knees that puts God in His rightful place and us in ours. It is possibly the most appropriate physical response we can have toward a holy God. Kneeling can be a great way to show humility and can be effective in helping our bodies express sorrow over sin and our need for forgiveness. Like raising the hands, it is a position of surrender. One day every knee will bow; it's good to practice now.

Shouting (Ps. 5:11; Ps. 47:1)

People love to shout! In some cultures it is very common. We tend to be much more reserved in North America, but sporting events and rock concerts surely indicate that it's not at all a foreign concept to us. Shouting surely says something of the victory that is ours in Christ. When we do it in worship it is a great reminder of what God has done for all of us who have gathered in His name. Shouting and cheering is a natural and appropriate human response to things that are exciting and exceptional. What is more exceptional than that the God we've betrayed would come near to us through the blood of Christ? What is more exciting than living to see God's will being done on Earth as it is in Heaven? (Do I hear crickets?)

Clapping (Ps. 47:1)

Though only mentioned once in Scripture, I always say, "How many times would God have to put it in there for us to do it?" Now, it is always great fun to try to get a bunch of white people to clap to the beat. (Hey, I'm as white as they come!) I've laughed out loud more than once when leading. However, clapping doesn't have to be just on the beat. Some people can't, so let them go nuts and let's enjoy their exuberance anyway. There is also clapping as applause. I've had to deal with a few people on this who were adamant that there should be no applause in church. It's useless to argue, better to just go ahead and do it. When teaching a church to applaud in worship we must make sure to state that we are not clapping for excellent performances, as if clapping for people on stage; we are clapping because our hearts are celebrating who God is and what He's done. We're saying, yes and amen - we couldn't agree more with what we've just sung. This is a totally appropriate response, and it reminds us of the presence of the King.

Dancing/ Jumping (Ps. 105:4; Ps.149:3)

I've also taken heat on this form of worship, but the reality is we were designed by God to move to Him and to move to music. My small children love to dance and worship as I play songs on my guitar. They jump around singing, "pwaise the Lo!" (Praise the Lord) Worship doesn't get much more pure than that. Though this is something that may cause angst in different church environments, we have biblical reasons and permission to do so. As in all the forms, I'm not saying you have to start this week, but do begin to train your people to be accepting and not judging. Then they will be ready if and when something like this should come into the service.

Singing/ Music (Ps. 21:13; Ps. 66:23; Ps. 104:33; Mk. 12:30 Deut. 6:4; Heb. 8,9)

Yes, music is a wonderful from of worship. Nothing is probably so universal a stimulus as music. Most everyone likes some style of music. Raising our voice to sing to the King has, for generations, and for millions of God followers, been a key outlet for tangibly experiencing the intangible. Every move of God produces a new catalogue of worship music. Sadly, new expressions are often scowled at by the previous generation, who are determined that their music is the music of heaven. It takes maturity to welcome the new as well as to preserve the best of the old and take it forward as the continuing language of worship.

Another part of music is the craft of using it to lead worship. You've probably been in services where the leader felt they had to say something after every song. Sometimes leaders get into an annoying habit of stopping and praying after every song. Some leaders never say anything; they just sing. Worship through singing means more than just being a song leader. If you're a leader, study great worship leaders to discover how to engage people in worship as they sing.

Banners (Ps. 20:5; Ex. 17:15; Is. 11:10, Zech. 9:16)

Banners can have multiple uses, either stationary or active. We understand from a patriotic perspective the importance of the flag. Spiritually it is even more significant, that God goes before us, that His name is high above us. Some people find the movement of flags in worship to be very celebrative. We understand this at sporting events. There is nothing new under the sun here, and so can be embraced as a legitimate expression of worship.

Incense (Ps. 141:2)

Another sensory stimulus, there was a special incense in Bible times that could only be used in the temple. People would experience and associate a certain smell with the house of God. Allergy considerations aside, incense can set a very nice ambience for worship.

Removal of shoes (Ex. 3:5)

We all know the story of Moses at the burning bush. Odor-eaters aside, this one may not do the trick for everyone. But I know several people who find it very meaningful to enjoy the symbolism of worshipping this way. Moses was told the ground He was standing on was holy. His response to take off his Nikes was God-directed. But remember, Moses did not know God at all at this first encounter. We know God and so let's feel free to respond without being told to. Again, freedom in worship needs to become a prized value in our churches. Each person may wish to do things uniquely as they express themselves to God. Let's foster that and encourage people to meet with God and use expressions of various types. If we view these forms with welcome instead of suspicion, the whole tone of worship will change.

Meditation (Ps. 119:97; Ps. 1:2; Josh. 1:8; Ps. 19:14)

The word is such a high value for God honoring worship. We need to spend time just soaking in the Scriptures. We should spend time just reading it in silence, perhaps up on the screen. This is both a staple of our personal devotion and our corporate worship devotion. Try putting up Scripture and then put questions up on the screen that help people interact with the passage.

Fasting (Matt. 6:16-18; I Cor. 7:5; II Cor. 6:5)

A people hungry for revival can do this in community and watch God pour out His Spirit. I've also personally been blessed by times of fasting, as the absence of food reminds me of my dependence on God. You can bet that when you eat again after a day or a few of fasting, your prayer of thanks will be a lot more heartfelt, rather than a 10 second "sudden migraine" prayer. (Like the ones some people do when they eat at McDonalds and don't want anyone to know they're praying.)

Prayer – We could call this practicing the presence of God. (Matt. 6:9-13; Ps. 17:6; Ps. 141:2)

When Jesus was on earth He repeated God's Old Testament desire that His house should be a house of prayer. Yet many church services today include less than 2 minutes of prayer. Jesus' disciples asked Him to teach them to pray. It would be helpful to re-teach this to our churches and raise the value of prayer. Prayer should not always be done from the platform. This is a great opportunity to include the congregation in worship.

The Lord's Prayer, in Matthew 6:9-13 gives us some direction. We should be praying:

- For God's glory to be manifest (His attributes on display).
- Acknowledging His rightful place in our lives and in worship.
- For the renown and reverence of His name.
- That struggling Christians would surrender their hearts and resources to God.
- That Jesus would be the central focus of worship.
- That Christians would be passionately spreading God's Kingdom.
- That true worship will ascend to God from pure hearts
- For the Holy Spirit to work in lives, giving victory over sin.
- For purification in the body/ for spiritual depth.
- For growth among the saints to be conformed to the image of Christ.

- Prayers confessing personal and corporate sin
- For God's will to be done.
- For the salvation of the lost.
- Pray for government leaders.
- Pray for church leaders.
- Bearing one another's burdens to the Father.
- Prayers of praise.
- Prayers of thanksgiving.

Our prayers in corporate worship are to be a lot more outward focused than self-centered. (Matt 6:7,8)
Ask your church these questions as you make prayer a greater focus in worship:

- Why is it so important that we exalt God in prayer?
- Why does God want us to pray to Him?
- What will an intense focus on God in our prayer and worship produce?

Public Reading of Scripture (I Timothy 4:13)

Just like prayer, the word is in short supply in many churches today. Not only do few people even carry a Bible to church with them anymore, they wouldn't need to open it if they did because there are so many services being conducted without any *word* whatsoever. We as a church need to love the word of God. It should be up on the screens in our worship times, perhaps in between verses of a song, or for a time of responsive reading. We can put it up for a time of reflection on a passage. Whatever we think our people need, the reality is they probably need more of the word than they are currently getting. And it doesn't count to simply say, "Well, our worship was Bible based." Prove it! Preachers, don't merely claim your sermons are biblical; actually use the Bible!

Silence (Ps. 46:10; Ps. 37:7; Mk. 6:31)

Sometimes the best way to start a worship service is in complete silence. We don't have much time for silence in our busy lives. We don't like silence because it often betrays the fact that we are empty people. We use busyness to cover up unfulfilled longings that only Christ can meet. Many people complain that they cannot hear God's voice. Is there any relation between the amount of noise we fill our lives with and the feeling that God doesn't talk to us? Lovers of God love times of silence. They hear His voice in the silence. It is an exercise worth leading your people into in worship. Maybe 30 seconds is all they can handle at first. But eventually they will learn that silence in worship is not awkward; it is a time when God speaks.

Offering (Ps. 96:8; Matt. 5:23,24)

Other than having been reduced to something so perfunctory, the offering is usually looked over as an element of worship. We are supposed to bring our offerings to God. Perhaps the best thing we can do for a while is stop passing the plates and have people come forward to kneel and present their offering at the altar. We need not be afraid of talking about tithes and preaching about offerings in the pulpit. It is easy to say Jesus is Lord, but the area of the wallet is often the last area of surrender to become subject to the rule and reign of God.

The Lord's Supper (1 Cor. 11:23 cf, Lk. 22:14cf)

Like the offering, communion is often done as such a lifeless ritual that we miss the opportunity for a vital meeting with God. There are more ways to do it than just passing the bread and the cups down the rows. Have people come forward to stations where they can take both elements back to the seats and partake together. Or have the elements passed out and serve the person beside you. Or have people stand up and come and tear a piece of bread and dip it in the wine rather than drink it.

Regardless of the form, make it meaningful. Have people quote or read their favorite verses while the elements are being passed. Every time communion is done there should be a different take on it. Use multiple passages over the course of the year to drive at different aspects of communion, such as extending forgiveness to others, confronting a brother who has sinned against you, the need to confess our sins and examine ourselves, the fact that Jesus is waiting for us to come home and won't take communion again until He does so in the Kingdom of God. (Matt 26) There are so many ways to set up communion. It is for shame that some churches do it the same way *every* time. Some pastors even use the same Scripture and say the same words every time. How is that different from the vain repetition and vain ritual that Jesus and the prophets spoke so vehemently against?

Visual Arts/ multi-media

We live in a world that is visually oriented. The use of video and image is key to communicating kingdom truth and can really set up response through song. There are some excellent resource videos out there. At this point in time I'm only aware of a few websites that offer videos that are truly worship oriented. (There are many great videos on other themes) There is a whole opportunity out there to be tapped for some gifted graphic artists to put together some stunning videos incorporating the names and attributes of God, calls to worship and more.

Candles/ alternate lighting

Similarly, because we are sensory creatures, lighting can set a mood, which can be used to draw focus to the various elements of worship. I've observed that worshipping in a dimly lit setting can actually be very conducive to letting the walls come down in people's hearts. They are more likely to let go and be broken before the Lord when they don't have bright lights shining on them. I know many people, myself included, who love the sense of being able to let the tears fall in worship without worrying about who's looking around.

Baptism (Romans 6:1-14)

Baptism is one of the high-water marks (pun intended) of living out obedience to Christ. It is something that we should celebrate and can lend to wonderful times of exhilarating praise. We're talking about life coming up out of the grave, for crying out loud! Make it memorable; make it meaningful.

Testimonies of God's works (Ps. 78:1-7; Ps. 22)

If there is one thing the mature in the faith are called to do, it is to worship by modeling a life of worship to the next generation. If you want to pass on the forms of worship to the next generation, you may be sorely disappointed at how little they want to take with them, but your experience of God can encourage and inspire an entire generation of young worshippers when you share what God has done for you. Worship through testimony is the act of one generation passing onto the next their *experience* of the faith. Sadly, there are many who have attended church all their lives and come close to the end, realizing that they have nothing to pass on because they have not walked with God closely. How sad to be of age and see both your beloved forms and your legacy vaporize because they both lack context.

A dear elderly saint in our church just recently shared her testimony of how she grieved the death of three grown children in three different events. There must not have been a dry eye in the place. Her story of hope, healing and learning to praise God in the midst of these horrific losses is what we're talking about. Not everyone experiences something so traumatic in their lifetime, but we have a whole generation coming up who need to hear from seventy year-olds how hard it was to stay pure when they were twenty; to deal with loss of a job and loss of loved ones; to go through seasons when God seemed silent; to share how God called them out of darkness into His marvelous light.

Weeping/ Lament (Psalms/Lamentations)

Most people think praise when they think Psalms, but did you know that eighty-four percent of the Psalms are written in the context of trouble, calamity and lament? Either the psalmist is seen as calling out to God in the middle of trouble, or thanking God for relief from trouble, or asking God to spare Him from trouble in most of the Psalms. It is not ironic. Worship and praise for us occur in the midst of the "stuff" (or insert your own word) of everyday life! We don't see the ideal, only reality. Sometimes reality bites. But God is still worthy of praise. So we need to allow times, especially when the church family is grieving a loss, to let our worship be guided through lament. We need to be directed to appropriately respond to God through the Psalms. A good friend of mine recently shared how the church came together and lamented in worship at the tragic loss of their senior pastor's daughter. There is something powerful in building community and sharing grief and sorrow in a way that still considers the hope and consolation of Christ.

Observation of nature (Psalm 19; Romans 1:19,20)

Some people, men especially, find themselves able to connect with God better out in nature rather than in a sterile sanctuary. God can meet us powerfully in the outdoors, and creation tells us a lot about our Maker. There are many creative ways that we can use images and references to nature in corporate worship that will strongly connect with people.

Poetry/ Writing

Some people express themselves to God best on paper through writing, painting or drawing. This is something you can encourage both in private and corporate worship as a perfectly legitimate form of worship. How do you think we got our Psalms? I doubt they were all prayers that got prayed and then the author said to himself, "Quick, I've got to write that one down!" If God wrote us a big letter, why can't we write Him one? My father-in-law is a prolific note-taker in worship. He never sings, but he is a true worshipper.

A word to the wise on introducing new elements/ change etc...

Worship is supposed to be the unifying factor in a church. Sadly often it is the dividing factor. Know that your church's worship is a reflection of what God has done in your midst. Sometimes we need to ask ourselves, is the "capital B" battle worth fighting in my church? At some level there is an understanding, even a sad resigning to the fact that God's Spirit may not be welcome in your present church. God may need new wineskins to do His work, because the old would burst under the duress of change. Enter into seasons of change under advisement. If this is really where God wants your church to go, then the leadership of the church needs to be totally unified. If not, you are setting yourself up for the battle of your life – and soul. I speak as one who has been called into these situations for my entire ministry career thus far. Brothers and sisters, if this is not 100 percent the call of God for you to do, then step back now. In the dark months and even years ahead as you face opposition to change and worship renewal, you will need to remember that God called you to this. If He did not, you will not be able to withstand.

So be advised on the rate of change. We so often wish we could just press the reset button on our church and fix everything and restore things to Kingdom values with the snap of the fingers. If that is God's plan, He'll probably call you to a church plant, where you can start from scratch and set the values and the DNA afresh. If not, then realize that the journey, the struggle, the unlearning that is going to happen in your church is God's plan for creating mature disciples. You can be absolutely right in your view, but dead wrong in the way you wield it; you can be truthful as the day is long, but still be unrighteous.

Know your senior pastor and leadership. If you are the senior pastor, know your congregation and fellow church leaders. Get together off-site to know each other's hearts.

Don't just let your only time together be around the boardroom table. Be sure that the mission, vision, values of the church and the DNA will support worship renewal and change.

If you can assure people that your commitment to the word of God is as strong as ever and that it's okay to grieve loss, you can shepherd your people through transition and not have a bunch of bodies in the rearview mirror. Pray, seek the Lord. Be prepared to receive and respond in a gentle, but firm way to criticism. Be prepared to lose some people who are consumer Christians, or who are simply not mindful of the things of the Kingdom of God. But be careful to nurture and run after genuine saints who may feel left behind. Their faith stories are the treasure your body needs to give it context to the new work of God. There are genuine, godly saints who will struggle with change. Nurture them; spend time with them. Explain it to them patiently again and again. Create opportunities for the old and the younger innovators to get to know each other in off-site settings.

This community building and trust is essential. Change coming from people with whom you have relationship is easy compared to when it feels like people you don't even know are imposing it on you. I've seen this in a few situations, where an older man will be spending time talking to a young teen, maybe giving some advise, or just praying with him. A few months later, this young teen is up playing drums in church. That same old man is now not thinking, "those young people and their irreverent music;" he's thinking, "Isn't it wonderful that young Adam is up there serving the Lord. I don't care much for the music, but it's great that he's serving." There was a man in my last church who would often say, "I don't care for the music, but I love the worship!" Another gem of a saint who "got it!"

In my own life I've found that some of the most resistant people to change in worship and music are instantly softened when I offer to go rake their leaves or put firewood in for them. They invite me in for hot cocoa and cookies after; we chat for a few moments. They are grateful that I would take the time to help. The next time I see them after a worship service they go out of their way to share with me how meaningful they found the worship time. I'm thinking, "I didn't do anything different," but relationship helps people process change. I wish this kind of successful bridge-building was common, but I share this as an example of those precious times when a connection is made.

What do we do, though, when truly God-loving saints are struggling and really grieving over change? First, let's remember to delineate between two kinds of change. One is the correcting of heart and focus we want to bring to worship, which no one who loves the Lord and word of God will dispute. For these people, it means reminding them of the un-changing purpose of the church and how they can leave a godly legacy.

But the other kind of change is the change of methods. Unfortunately both changes in mechanics and in focus often happen at once. That is often because churches resist change for so long, and then realize they are dying. They carry on in ignorant bliss, "solid on the Rock." They don't notice the church getting older and it's like they wake up one morning and realize they have no young families, only 2 teenagers, and the average age of attendees is now sixty-four. They are faced with the reality of "change or die." This is practically the kiss of death. They then quickly try to make changes to save the church, but because they have not fostered change as a normative attitude of a growing, healthy church, people balk at it and churches split and other ugly stuff happens. It would be lovely to be able to renew focus without bringing in drums or tearing out the pews, but the reality is that if the focus had been right all along, the correct changes would have gradually been introduced over the years, causing virtually no headaches. Instead of prevention medicine, churches are often faced with invasive, inconvenient and tortuous surgery.

Model the change you seek

The simple truth is that you can want change, you can give permission to break out in worship, but until the leaders and pastors of a church take steps of faith in modeling the forms of worship, your people will smell a fraud. This is not about mechanical changes; it is about heart change. People need to see that God is working revival in leadership if they are to follow. And, as I said above, if change is to come, it will work best when it comes from the people rather than being imposed on the people. So lead people to the place of drawing correct conclusions on their own. There is no formula here, sorry. Just know that when people's lights go on, they will soon be the ones leading you in worship as spontaneous praise may well erupt in worship. Perhaps the best thing you as church leadership can do is direct people to get into other worship settings where freedom is being modeled. Maybe this means sending twenty of your people to a worship conference. Maybe it starts by partnering with other churches in town to do combined praise gatherings where they can rub shoulders with some not-so-frozen-chosen.

Chapter 7
Balance in Worship

When I was growing up, health nuts said fat was the enemy in our diet. Then it was cholesterol, then just trans fats. Now it seems like the fad is to get rid of carbs. Of course, experienced nutritionists have had it right all along: Everything in moderation – even French-fries. It's about healthy, intentional balance. One of the hardest things in life is balance. We must also walk the line in our corporate worship gatherings. Here are several pairs that I have found necessary to balance.

Reverence and Jubilation

History is replete with traditions that put too much emphasis on one side of our corporate experience of God to the neglect of the other. Yes, we fear God; Yes, we show appropriate respect in His presence. But some would go so far as to say that things like laughter and applause and blue jeans are inappropriate for the house of God. Another side of this would be to say that only the professional ministers can run a worship time. Both of these challenge our biblical right as priests under our great High Priest and the access to the Father that He has given us by which we can come boldly. Is there is a reason why even in this modern day western world you can take a group of perfectly normal people, stuff them into a sterile sanctuary, and this sedated state of perpetual long-faced religion ensues? What ever happened to the joy of the Lord and the abundant life that Jesus promised for the here and now? Why must our worship services be so boring, so irrelevant, so prone to façade, and so devoid of the Holy Spirit's power, transformation, and blessing?

Let's be fair to caution the other side of the issue as well. There is a healthy place for examining ourselves, particularly in relation to the Lord's Supper. In some faith traditions it is all celebratory to the point of fakeness, where lament is not welcome, where superficiality is a higher objective than transparency.

To bring some balance then, the reality is that just as our personal lives have seasons, so does the body of Christ. There are times when whole services should focus on repentance and contrition, and yet with the offer of hope. And there ought to be times when the spirit of celebration is fostered and encouraged, yet with the reminder that our ability to celebrate cost our Savior dearly.

Pink and Blue

There is an excellent book out there called "Why Men Hate Going to Church," by David Murrow. In it he talks about the fact that so much of what church has become is un-appealing to men. We soft sell Jesus as a wimp when we focus on one part of His nature to the exclusion of others. Lets start with our sanctuaries: Pretty, flowery, comfy; that's one side of Jesus. Think about our sermons: mercy, grace, joy, compassion; that's one side of it. Think about our songs: beauty, love, desire, know, affection, tender, touchy; that's one side of it. Do you see what I mean? So much of our church and worship experience caters to a more feminine viewpoint. As a result, men increasingly feel like Jesus is irrelevant, and even a pansy. What of a God of wrath? A warrior? A King? A conqueror? Having all authority and coming to judge and reign? Lion of Judah? You see, even women find these attributes appealing. Why do we have so many churches that feel and even smell more like funeral parlors than maybe a pub, where men naturally are drawn? In our worship experiences we need to put all of God on display and let Him put us in awe. We don't need a sanitized, pushover God; we need the real deal. Let's stop shying away from, ignoring, or making excuses for the things in God that are not "safe." Lets make sure that our worship language is more inclusive of what men are experiencing as well.

Planned and Spontaneous

This one can be humorous at times, especially when I look back at spontaneous things I've seen that ended up being gong shows, and even on planned times that simply were counter-intuitive.

God is a God of order, yes. I get reminded of this often when I make a last minute change or stray off the "program" in leading worship. And He is also glorified by the heart's intent. So here's the balance: To those who think all planning should be thrown out the window, because "God will not be confined by our schedule," let's not assume that the Lord was not consulted in the process of laying plans. Understand instead that He is glorified by diligence in preparation and our seeking to effectively communicate to the flock. Conversely, let's hold an understanding that our best laid plans may need to be put aside from time to time. Here is a common illustration of this:

There are a number of times that I've been vexed at transitions from myself to a preacher. Many times I'll bring a service down to a reflective moment and the preacher, rather than taking it further and seizing a shepherding moment for leading or praying over the people, will jump right into his pre-programmed punch line – usually some attempt at humor. This insensitivity is a missed opportunity at best and may be at times quenching the work of the Spirit. Let's always ask ourselves as leaders and pastors, "Am I aware of what has just happened before me?" Let's avoid treating our part of the service in a vacuum as if it is the only part of the service and nothing has happened before we took to the platform.

Flow and Function

Similarly, think in terms of, "we have some things we need to include in today's service" vs. "we must interject these things at all cost, not matter how awkward it feels in the service." It may be appropriate to tell the congregation about the tragic death of a church member and funeral arrangements. But do you do that right before you sing "Lord I lift your name on High?" It might be wonderful to let everyone know about Aunt Margaret's 90th birthday party, but do you do that just after leading a time of repentance? It might be necessary to take up the morning offering, but do you have to crack a joke about it, or could it be more God focused? Does a separate person have to mount the platform to pray for the offering, or could the worship leader do it, or better still, have several in the congregation offer up prayers of thanksgiving to God right on the spot? Standing and greeting and interacting with other worshippers might have its place, but why does it always seem to be placed immediately after we've drawn people to a focal point in worship? Again, we have 167 other hours a week to meet with people and hang out. And I can't count the number of times a holy moment has been kicked in the teeth by a poorly placed joke or an insensitive, bombastic transition from the sublime to the trivial. I've seen it where people have audibly been weeping and doing business with God in a worship time, and some leader will get up and say, "Would you stand and greet one another." I'm sure heaven cringes. We do have things that need to happen in the life of the body when everyone is together, but how can you create continuity for people rather than send distraction bombs into the service, jerking around from one thing to the next in ADD style?

Revelation and Response

It is interesting that one of the critiques of much modern worship is the "lack of content." Accusations of romanticizing, egotistical music, and flawed or weak theology have their validity. Some would even consider it insipid. (And we seek to address some of that in other places in this book.) But what really is often happening is that revelation and response are out of balance. The opposing problem is one of "information download and thus overload" that lacks context for my daily walk with God. Many of us have been in services that felt just plain rigid and bulletin driven. The "so what" question never gets answered. There is no opportunity to pause and let my heart soak in and begin to process all that I have just heard. Pastors often cancel out the power of their good point by jumping to the next one too soon. How about a moment of silence to let the tension of the moment be felt? This is more than just a good homiletic technique that I'm trying to get at here. Are there better ways to help our people devotionally interact with the principles that are being taught?

A good service nourishes the whole person- the mind, the heart, and sees the body's senses as the intermediary between the two, which is where forms of worship come in. All the tools that we've talked about in this book are ways to help the heart deal with what we are learning. The three-part revelation/response worship approach that I like to use works well here: first, seeing God as He is; second, seeing ourselves for who we are; and third, gaining a passion for what is on God's heart.

Truth and Feeling

It is important to remember that Jesus came full of grace and truth. We as leaders seeking to create Kingdom-loving Christ followers have got to apply the grace of God to His unchanging truth when we deal with people's hearts and lives. Truth often hurts, but sometimes people will push aside truth without love. If we just lay down the truth without acknowledging the real life circumstances that people come to worship with, we actually encourage superficiality. Let's not be afraid to let our people "feel" as well. We use Scripture to guide feelings and to correct people when feelings cause wrong thinking and actions. That approach is probably better that laying down cold truth and saying, "Now make your feelings fit inside this concrete mold." Balance in worship means we keep unchanging truth *and* we at some level allow people to let the Holy Spirit guide them rather than expecting everyone's journey and expression of worship to be a carbon copy of others.

Familiar and Unfamiliar

You've probably been in worship situations where the songs were all unfamiliar, the flow was different than you've experienced etc... If you're visiting a new setting you might be prepared to expect that. It's a little more disconcerting when it's your home church and you realize that everything familiar has been taken away. It is hard to enter in with unfamiliar forms. Of course there is nothing wrong with new forms, just that we have to be measured in our implementation of them.

Creating some discomfort is probably good at times. Perpetual instability is not so good. One of the pastors I've worked with compares people to rubber bands. They will stretch to a point, but then you've got to relax the tension, then push again. A limbered up elastic band will stretch further in the end than one just taken out of the bag and put into such action. So again, balance is needed. The Scripture exhorts us in the use of the "new song," which I take to be both literal and figurative. One speaks of the continual transformational work of God which is new as we experience His mercy every morning. And it's natural then that as each generation finds this to be so, they must find new ways to express this in song. Let's not exasperate our people with new songs. Particularly if you're a musician, you'll find that your appetite for new songs is about 3 times that of the average churchgoer. In this case, when you're sick of a song, the church is probably just starting to get on to it. This is when you worship by *serving* the congregation, patiently waiting for them to learn songs and other means.

Stage and Congregation

There is no question that the stage is a "form" in our culture. We pay attention to those on stage. We observe; we become spectators; we idolize. That can be a really bad thing when it comes to the priesthood of believers and the participatory nature of worship that we should be seeking. Some of our facilities are so constructed that they might just as well have a sign that says, "This is a great place to watch something happen on the stage." We can certainly utilize well-designed worship spaces, but let's make sure that they are designed for worship. I've been in over a hundred sanctuaries in my touring ministry all the way from 40-seat to 5,000-seat auditoriums. Almost none of them are designed with kneeling in mind. Similarly, then, there's not much room to dance or even sway a little. What does that communicate to people? You're here to watch the pros. You can sing if you want, but we on stage are the main draw. (Insert motion sickness bag here! That's just not right!) Some of us have inherited facilities where we are going to have to work super hard to make sure that the congregation feels not just part of the service, but that we on stage draw worship out of them by facilitating services where congregational input comes to be expected.

Engaging people and Staying out of the way

There is a tension when the arts are used in worship that people will either be led so tightly in an experience that they don't get to express themselves, or they are led so loosely that there is anarchy. We as leaders and pastors sometimes have to prompt the people, but we should never have to beg them to worship. The worship leader should want so much for people to see only Jesus, but at the same time, that will be accomplished as we lead with confidence and give appropriate direction. Things like getting people clapping or telling them where the song is going next as they sing are helpful. It is a somewhat subjective art to ensure that people are engaging with God and not just responding to your charisma on stage. This is not about manipulation; it is about trying to draw out of people what God is doing in their hearts and what He wants to do in their hearts.

The flipside of this balance coin needs to be given consideration too, though. I've been in too many situations where the person leading worship was so inept and unskilled that all we could see was their insecurity and uncertainty of where the song is going, or what comes next. That has just as negative an affect as the worship leader who evidences narcissism on stage.

Encouraging Giving and Receiving from Worshippers

We have a great God who has done all the giving, and in Scripture He calls the thirsty, the hungry, the poor, lame and naked to come to Him for what we all so desperately need. The balance then, is that we don't come to worship just to receive. The Scripture is clear that we are bringing an offering - to give and to bring praise to the Lord in the assembly. When we err on the side of too much receiving we run the risk of becoming worship consumers, always looking for our favorite song or that special thing to happen that will do it for us. If we come with an aversion to displaying need and only to give we run the risk of either believing that we have no need or that rather, God needs us. Or we'll be too ashamed to show that we have need because we feel that we should only worship in a giving mode. So worship leaders must make sure that people appropriately understand that

God wants to meet us in our need as we worship and also is worthy of receiving worship whether we feel like it or not.

Excellence and Authenticity

This is always a tough area to navigate, and it's often where people's feelings will get hurt. By excellence we do not mean perfection. Excellence is "how" we go about what we do. Excellence in worship honors God and inspires people. Lead worship with the stated purpose of having an unrelenting focus on our relationship with Christ, and remind your congregation of it often.

It seems to me that many smaller and even bigger churches seem inclined to put together worship teams "like the one we saw at the conference" or "like the other churches in town have." What makes churches think that they need a praise band? I've seen it too often where people with a pulse get put up on stage to do things they are not qualified to do. The result is a gong show. Any visitor would be embarrassed; any musician would cringe. Someone will say, "but if it's from their heart it's ok." That statement usually draws an "Amen" from well meaning bystanders. But I want to challenge that assumption on a few levels.

In I Corinthians 15, Paul writes about music (not even pertaining to worship), but in the sense of a trumpet or flute making an "uncertain sound" in calling warriors to battle. Paul essentially asks, if the sound is uncertain, who will know whether that trumpet blast is really a call to battle, or some 11 year old practicing a funeral dirge? There is a parallel to worship playing here: If a drummer can't keep time, but I'm being asked to clap, but I can't clap because I can't even find 2 and 4 because the drummer is trying to be flashy, but stinking at it, or so inept that he doesn't even know where 2 and 4 are, how can I sing or clap along? (How's that for a run-on sentence?) If a singer is off-tune, or the guitarist keeps butchering a well-known song, and we all know what it's supposed to sound like, what will be the result? We'll get frustrated because we want to engage, but someone keeps hitting us on the head with the hammer of ineptitude and then complains, "Why aren't you worshipping?" Music is a language. If the language is being spoken so poorly, I won't understand, much less know how to respond. Tell me again, mediocrity in the church reminds people of what kind of God? Why then, were the Levites instructed to play skillfully? It was with the hope that they would inspire hearts toward God through their excellence. We would scarcely pay a salary to an unlearned preacher to step into the pulpit to teach us the ways of God. We would only on really bad days hop on an airplane with a guy who "has a great heart," but can't actually fly!

Why then do we put up with such terrible sounds on the platform? Obviously the fear of hurting someone's feelings is a big factor, and in a church culture where edifying critique has been absent, it's no fun to be the monster who introduces such an actually loving concept. Another reason is because we have a misunderstanding that there must be music for worship. We need to worship, so therefore we need someone to play music, right? Hmmm... Yet another reason churches allow such poor music is that some people really think that Sunday morning is a great time for amateurs to gain experience playing in front of people. That's noble in intent but lacking in logic! You practice and prove yourself faithful in every other area of ministry before being given a significant public responsibility. Why should the ministry of worship be different?

This one is hard to balance, especially for those like me with professional ears. How much excellence is good enough for the King? I'll state this as questions that leadership at churches would do well to ask themselves.

- What can we in our church of 150, (or whatever number) realistically hope to achieve with our musicians?
- Can we put a few less people up there and in doing so lower the noise factor and actually raise the quality? (Does putting more people on stage really make things sound better?)
- Why do we have to sing to worship in the assembly? What other means should we try?
- Should we perhaps invest, as a church, in some of our young people to see that they get proper training to be the next generation of worship leaders and musicians?
- Can we partner with other churches to rub shoulders with their musicians and get ideas on how to improve?

So what about authenticity and character? This is the flip side. I have a friend who says it's a lot easier to train a musician to be a worshipper than to take a worshipper and train them to be a musician. True enough. It usually takes many years of discipline to make a skilled player, whereas someone can become an impassioned worshipper the moment they die to self. The character of those on stage is all-important, as I note elsewhere in this book. The reality is that worship leading and playing is a dual calling, not really a balancing act, so this point of balance is actually a trick point. Worship ministry is a call to a consistent walk with God *and* an ability to speak musical language.

Preference of the People vs. Intentionally Creating Some Discomfort

In the mass of any church we always have people far from God, people who know God and people who love God. Usually in worship we are leading people from every category at once. In I Corinthians particularly, Paul acknowledges that unbelievers are often present at church gatherings. We don't need to get into a deep debate here on what kinds of church in general we ought to have, (seeker oriented, seeker sensitive, believer only, etc...) for God uses them all to reach people. But we're talking specifically about a service of *worship* here. I do need to go on record as saying that as far as the worship goes, God only accepts worship from His children. (see 1 Cor. 2:14 -16; Psalm 50:16) The unsaved are unable to offer worship to God because they do not have His

Spirit living in them. So there is a sense in which some, even much of what we do in a worship service, will be inaccessible to the unsaved. That doesn't mean they are unable to attend, just that some of the discomfort we might sense from them or feel for them is the same that you would feel while sharing an intimate time around a different family. The people who should feel the greatest conviction in our services are probably the spiritually immature -the goats and the Pharisee's. But worship ought to make us uncomfortable; it ought to stretch us and convict us. We ought to be confronted with the choice to draw near or pull away from God.

Corporate and Personal

There has been a lot of recent attention to the problem of unhealthy individualism in the body of Christ. Many of these correctives have been very helpful because for far too long I have seen my church routine as something that is just "me and God," and nobody else needs to be there to make this work. *I* am saved and *I* am going to heaven. This mindset is hazardous to our spiritual health. We were made for earthly relationships. We were made with a need to do life and to do church together. So there is some good re-centering that has occurred in the emerging church in terms of using songs with plural rather than singular pronouns, for example. Things like fostering a greater sense of community and practicing the "one anothers" of Scripture are great. But like anything else, we are prone to extremes, and that being said, I want to send a small word of caution that we don't swing so far the other way in this collective mindset that we forget that salvation and our walk with God are first *personal*, not corporate in nature. He forgives *my* sins, then *we* can sing about how he washed *us* clean. He is the one *I* have chosen to live for, and I have joined with others who declare that *we* want to live for Him. *We* have come to worship and *I* have come to worship are *both* appropriate and should both be used. *We* should worship as community and *I* also need to cultivate worship alone in the quiet place with my Lord. He died for *me* and He died for *us*. Once again this not either/or, it is both/and.

I hope you see a common thread here; balance is hard but necessary work as we seek to lead our people. Perhaps you can think of other areas that need to be balanced in your situations.

Chapter 8

Developing Criterion for the Elements of Worship

Our songs must proclaim biblical, worshipful truth

I remember the day that I first made an issue about this in my home church. I was nineteen, and just off my first year of Bible College. I had lots of zeal and maybe not quite a full knapsack of tact. Thankfully, on this day it didn't matter; I was almost the youngest person there, and fondly loved by all the dear old people at our forty-person evening service. I was playing piano as another man was leading the hymns. Someone requested, "I've Got a Mansion Over the Hilltop." I got to the end of the first verse and stopped cold. There was a moment of awkward silence, and I felt that God was telling me to speak to the issue. We were singing a song about "me" and "what *I'm* expecting to be given to me when *I* get to heaven." I gave a little spiel on why this was not a worship song and how instead, we should be singing *to* Jesus. An old lady piped in, "Timothy, your grandmother would have said the same thing." Well, that was easy - except that my pastor came to my school the next day over lunch hour to speak to me about it. He was kind about it, but obviously concerned about the ripples this would cause. In his experience, he realized he hadn't done much thinking about the intent and potential of real Christ focused worship. Unfortunately, that church I grew up in had bigger problems than that as the years went on, and never did come to embrace worship and the pursuit of God. Instead, it became the kind of place that felt that it had the right views on this and that, thinking that others churches were inferior in their knowledge. Reliance on and passion for God was replaced with an unhealthily incessant level of study. The doors of that church are now closed. They had forgotten their first love and God removed their lampstand.

And so as much as this section may ruffle some feathers, we may need to do a serious overhaul of the kinds of songs we sing in worship. I had a dear old godly lady once approach me after a service and say, "O dearie, you just keep ruffling those feathers. Old fogies like me need to be jolted out of our complacency." Wow! Did she ever get it! That's one for the treasure box.

And so, for example, we may need to dismiss some songs that we have always just used. Perhaps every church would do well to do some spring-cleaning to their song catalogues. What follows here are some guidelines that may provide a springboard for discussions in your local church. Remember, not every song is appropriately focused for worship. That doesn't make it a bad song, and that doesn't make it fit for the pit, but if we want to be intentional about crafting a worship time that is God-focused, it will mean intentionally moving some songs to categories other than for a Christo-centric worship time.

Songs should allow the worshipper to focus on the character and nature of God and often give the worshipper opportunity to sing *to* God. Personalized music (I, me, my) is necessary; we must use personal pronouns in order to speak *to* God. This is not necessarily egocentric. Most great worship songs are songs where *I* am talking *to* God, extolling, exalting. In the case of the song above, it was not because the song was in first person that it got the axe; it was because there was no speaking *to* God, only about "me." There are some songs which are way over the top, like the one I just mentioned, in terms of "what I want" or "what I'm feeling," or "what I'm going to do" etc...

So use discretion to decide how much of *me* there should be in worship. You may decide that a song like "Trading My Sorrows" is too much that way. Maybe it's ok in some settings. I'm just trying to get us to think about the songs we sing here. "I Come to the Garden Alone" is considered by some to be an amazing hymn, but looking at it objectively, it seems to me that it is based not on worship, but on someone else's experience of worship, and therefore excludes other worshippers. Now, I'm not about to set out exhaustive lists of black and white listed songs. You and your church leaders should be working through it and wrestling with it. So, if it seems that you find that your catalogue is so heavy on "me" that we don't speak to God, there may be a problem. Similarly, if we only have songs that talk about God, but never allow "me" to interact with God, there may be an out of balance exclusion that forgets that

God is not just transcendent, but close to us and wanting a two-way relationship with us. A general rule of thumb here would be to stick to the psalm model, which often has me speaking directly to God.

Most of our hymnbooks contain personal "story" type songs. These are songs of Christian testimony, songs that tell a story, but with more of a narrative feel. Sometimes this is expressed in the second person as in, "Let me tell you a story." Narrative songs can be useful, and we're all for testimony. But testimonies are personal, and so unless the song is coming at it from the standpoint of, "God, you've been so good to *us*...," it probably is not helpful for us to sing about it in corporate worship. Yes, we are encouraged by testimony, but we don't need to recite other people's personal testimonies. It is important that songs are accessible to the broad congregation. Some songs are so explicitly based on one person's experience with God to the point that they can create disconnect with others trying to use that same language.

At any rate, a song needs to intentionally facilitate the next step toward communion/ relationship with God. They need to move us closer, not distract. Again, if we talk too much about "me and you," or we are addressing other people with our singing, we are falling off course. Songs like "They Will Know We Are Christians By Our Love," and "I'll Tell the World I'm a Christian" or "There's Power in the Blood" may well have their place in the general Christian experience, just not for worship. Any time we use songs *about* us rather than *to* God we run the risk of having taken our eyes off of Jesus. Ironically, the song, "Turn Your Eyes upon Jesus" may not be a great choice for worship since it's talking to people as an exhortation. Again, I think this is a wonderful song. It might be better incorporated as a call to worship or something like that. You see, this exclusive focus on God and God alone in worship is a lot harder than you might think because so many "good" things and "good songs" will get in the way; things that are not wrong, but not intentional enough in scope.

When we are putting together a worship service, we need to always ask some questions, like:

What are people trying to say to God? (What are people experiencing in their walk with Him?)

How can we select songs or Scriptures that evoke worship from the body? Keeping in mind the corporate *ethos* on a given week? How can we facilitate a personal God encounter in the corporate setting? How do we let the walls come down? What should people be dwelling on in worship?

How can we let the word of God speak?

We must keep God's word central in worship. If the worship time sets up a preaching time, how do we facilitate that? If the worship time is a response to the word, how do we facilitate response? Are we teaching and personalizing doctrine as we lead in worship? (We'd better be!) We need to worship with the spirit and with understanding. (I Cor. 14:15) Worship leading has a strong teaching component, which is why someone who sings well is not a fit worship leader on that merit alone.

Are songs about topics other than worship of the Almighty fit for worship?

Songs need to be carefully evaluated as to whether they facilitate worship or divert glory that belongs to Christ. We need to do more to focus on Christ and jealously guard our times of worship. Patriotic holidays, mothers/father's day, special recognition of persons, etc... all run the risk of becoming idolatry, while other items simply keep the "worship service" from being a *worship* service. Now you see how we get to the ruffling of feathers! You will encounter opposition when you begin to re-evaluate your services in this light. That doesn't mean shy away from this purifying calling, just realize that when we understand and implement the exclusive and intentional, unrelenting focus on Christ in our worship services, we may encounter hostility from those who prefer "feel good" man-centered services as opposed to confrontation with our jealous God. Worship services are not to be about the business of promoting patriotism, politics, or honoring anyone other than Christ. "My country 'Tis of Thee" is not fit for worship; "America the Beautiful" is a nice song of sentiment toward the country, but it is not worthy to be compared with or put in place of worship directed toward our beautiful Savior.

Songs for worship should glorify persons of the Godhead and not point to objects or entities other than God. Now, here I will get my hands a bit dirty and give you a "black list" starter kit. Consider popular songs such as *The Old Rugged Cross, Church in the Wildwood, Mansion Over the Hilltop, America the Beautiful, I'll Fly Away, My Country 'Tis of Thee, God Save the Queen, Faith of our Fathers*, many Christmas carols and numerous others in our hymnbooks. They all need to be evaluated - as do the latest wave of new songs that talk about such erroneous concepts as God "needing" us or our praise, of God being limited, of God being spoken of with feminine pronouns, etc... These are just a few of the concepts creeping into modern hymnody that we must guard against. Songs about simply "good," "wholesome," "nice" themes are to be discounted, because they don't bring things down to the main point, which is the perfection of our God and how we can lay our lives and our love before Him. Songs suitable for hymn sings, or songs on general "Christian" topics are often not appropriately focused for the *worship* setting because they do not have a devotional connection that brings us to the feet of Jesus. Songs need to bring us back to the cross, back to our need, and we should live life from that place of worship.

Sentimental, traditional favorites and songs by famous writers carry no weight in determining their worth for use in the corporate worship of God. Just because a song appears in a hymnal, on a "Christian"' CD or has been accepted without question for years in a church or denomination does not make it acceptable for *worship*. Things that have been for a long time are in no way to be considered right on that basis alone. Widespread acceptance is not the benchmark of truth or rightness. As mentioned above, songs of Christian testimony/experience are not always appropriately focused for worship. Usually a refrain or chorus can determine this. A chorus can draw the previous material into a worship context, or lead it in a direction that altogether loses focus. In that sense a song like "Trading My Sorrows" leaves me in a toss-up, though I've used it. And I think a song Like "The Old Rugged Cross" would be worship worthy if only it had a different chorus. To be fair, my song, "Is Anybody Thirsty," is probably also on the fence. I've only ever used is as a call to worship. Sometimes we have to ask ourselves, "Where would this song fit in a worship time?"

We've talked a fair bit about music so far, but let's broaden this to include other elements of worship, which may include dramas, liturgies and prayers, testimonies, and others.

What should be our objectives for the components of worship?

What follows are some things that help us, as we as worship planners and leaders seek to help worshippers embrace the way of Jesus and honor God and His word. Note: Obviously we can't include all that follows in any one or even two services or it would be 12 hours long. (Hey, that might be fun!) These are guides for the themes that your church's worship should include, I would suggest, at least once a quarter. This is more of a general flavoring of how to make evaluation of whether our services are really *worship services*, or some other kind of miscellaneous church service.

We want our services to carry an intensity and immanent hunger in our personal relationship with God - a Holy dissatisfaction with status quo – a want to go deeper in our walk with God, desperation for revival. That's what our people need, a passion for Jesus. We do them a disservice by dumbing down worship and the word, or by candy coating and tickling the ears of the goats in our midst. There are things that goats hate, and quote me on this: it will be the goats that make noise when Jesus alone is the focus of worship. Enough of making everyone comfortable! Where do we get the idea that an encounter with the Living God, the All Consuming Fire, is a comfortable enterprise? He comforts the afflicted, that's true, but He unsettles the over-comfortable, self-reliant Pharisees. Try to find a time in Scripture where Jesus preached comfort to the Pharisees. I can't be so bold as to claim to know people's hearts. And only God knows whom the real (or should we say, fake) Pharisee's are. The point being, that the fruit will ultimately show us who's walking in step with the Sprit.

So we must make much of the exaltation and glorification of Christ in our corporate worship. Our worship must have an unrelenting focus on the preeminence of Christ, so that everyone will see that in God's true Churches, Christ is first in everything. (Col. 1:18) We must speak to Him, call upon His name, and allow the names and the attributes of God to lead us in pursuit of our Maker. Our worship should express a desire that all creation join in worship. This is about so much more than just our little church service! And even if your church is ten thousand strong, that's small compared to the whole Church. We are part of something much bigger than ourselves, and so our worship ought to have that *big* focus that we want to see every nation, tribe and tongue and the whole of creation bow the knee to the *King!*

Another facet of our worship is that we emphasize salvation through faith in the all-sufficient work of Christ apart from works. We should set out in worship to seek God's desire to glorify Himself in worship. This is not about you and me; it's about the incomparable glory of God, which we need to learn to chase and love more than life itself. How do you perpetuate a mediocre church when every heart is trained to live beyond themselves for the Glory and Kingdom of God? You can't! So if you like mediocrity, keep doing what you're doing. But know that worship with the focus on Christ will change your church. Passion for Christ and ineffective churches are simply not allowed in the same sentence. We're not talking about perfect little churches here, were actually talking about messed up churches made up of messed up people who all admit their messed-upedness. When that kind of humility pervades the church, you'll find the end of finger-pointing, whiny-pants, spoiled brat Christianity.

In worship we reflect a desire to humbly bring our offerings to God. This is not about watching an event on TV. Worship is about giving and bringing an offering. It is about coming prepared and ready to listen and change according to the promptings of the Holy Spirit. It is about the transformation of the worshipper. Our worship ought to invite God's Spirit to work in our own heart and in the assembly. We need to remind ourselves and our people of the simplicity, beauty, and centrality of Christ's gospel. Always. When we do this, we expose our absolute dependence on our God.

Our worship also ought to offer worshippers a future glory "high throne glimpse" of the worship of our King. The idea is to inspire and encourage people to love the coming of Jesus, to long for the day He takes the throne to reign forever.

Another objective is to encourage the worshipper to experience the tangible presence of God through holistic worship (heart, soul, mind and body). This is not yoga, it's what even the Hebrews understood in Deuteronomy 6 and Jesus repeated in the gospels. Ask yourself, how do we include people's intellect in worship? The heart? The senses? We recognize that worship is based first on fact and faith, but that emotions are also to be engaged in worship. Christ didn't just serve us up with a bunch of facts; He threw his strongest passions into it.

Our worship ought to allow us to rejoice and celebrate abundant life in Christ. (making His praise glorious, boisterous, joyful, even loud!) How do we bring the zeal of a professional sporting event into worship? How do people get so passionate, even violent about chasing a ball or a puck, but yawn, or show up late when it's time for Christ's glory to be put on display in the assembly? Maybe we need to ask ourselves why we put up with worship leaders and preachers who don't communicate this kind of passion for Christ – then again maybe we need to ask ourselves why we put up with people in the pews who just sit there and never engage. Maybe the solution is that we need to stop doing worship *for* them and actually begin to facilitate worship *from* them.

Another aspect of our corporate devotion is to reflect on God's faithfulness and mighty works past, present and future. Sometimes this can be done through personal testimonies of people and their "God stories." With the technology available today, even *America's shiest people* can be captured on DVD to share with the congregation. I've found testimony, especially in video, to be a powerful tool that personalizes theology and helps one generation to exult in front of another generation in God's faithfulness. And so worship is about us making our "boast" (holy pride) in the excellencies of God's character and nature. This is actually the meaning of the biblical word for *praise*!

And so as we worship we also want to encourage the worshipper to ask God to search the heart, to do His refining work, to purify His people. This means our worship ought to contain times of prompting repentance and seeking forgiveness. This is the experience of the cleansing of sin through confession. We want to be sure that our worship includes Godly sorrow and times of brokenness in the assembly. This transparency is very humbling and very healthy for the body as we reinforce that the ground around the cross is indeed level. Leaders and pastors and everybody else in our church may only approach the throne of God the exact same way.

Another big facet of worship is thanksgiving. We as leaders need to become champions for facilitating times where God's people revel in His victory, His provision, salvation, successes granted, and on and on. Part of our sinful nature is that we love to complain about all the stuff in life that stinks. Have you ever noticed that some people seem to complain incessantly, as if it were a way to make conversation? It is indeed a dialect of English for some. We need to make it known to our people that God has placed a premium on His people being different, namely in that they are constantly giving thanks to God, even in the most difficult seasons of life.

Worship declares our resolution and desire to follow God, to surrender to Him and obey His rule in all things. Someone once said that Christians tell more lies when they sing than any other time! But that shouldn't stop us from putting lyrics up on the screen in which the uncomfortable language of surrender is displayed. Worship puts words in our mouths; it invites us to say things and use words that we might not want to choose for ourselves, but that is exactly the point. Worship is about teaching our people to appropriately speak to God, modeling for them the things that they should be saying to Him in their daily prayer life and in times of corporate adoration.

We have talked about worship being our response. This was something highly advocated by the late Robert Webber in his teachings on worship. God reveals, we respond. He is always revealing and illuminating through the ministry of His Holy Spirit, and so we should always be responding. So we want to encourage the worshipper to respond to God's revelation, which we see happening in three main ways in Scripture: A)creation declaring and showing God to us, B)the word of God giving us instruction, encouragement and all that the word of God does, and finally, C) the revelation of Christ Himself. Responding to Christ is the perfection of worship, since the first two revelations are external stimuli that point us to the person of Christ, to whom we relate to and respond to. (Of course He is called the Word, and we respond to Him by obeying His word.)

Our God is a promise making, and more to the point, a promise keeping God. So let's have our worship times revel in His promises. He promises blessings to His children; He offers us the promise of His presence, His faithfulness and so on. In worship we would do well to remind our people of His promises and stand in awe as we see them all come true through the sum experience of the body at worship.

We've talked about transparency in worship, and so in addition to dealing with sin, worship at times can allow us to lay our hearts bare before Him, to be real and genuine with God, others and ourselves. We are a needy people; we are a hurting people. We are people in need of guidance; we are a sinful people. All of these should find voice and healing in the realized presence of God. And so we may also find that our worship calls on God for deliverance in the Christian life. We need victory over sin. We need comfort in persecution and in our circumstances. As we do this, let's make sure we magnify God and not our problems. We want to walk the line between us focusing on Him and appropriately bringing our personal needs to Him. Remember too, to walk the line of our corporate and personal worship. Worship should remind us that God only receives our worship in the context of right relationships with others.

Chapter 9
Implementation in the Real World

This is one of those chapters that I wished had been accessible to me thirteen years ago when I began leading worship in the local church. This gets down to some of the "nuts and bolts" everyday questions and issues on the "how."

Music:
Songs should be in language and styles accessible to the disciples of a church's primary culture.

The ancient Shakespearean language, for example, "eth" and "dst" endings, words whose etymology has changed and awkward idioms that are foreign in the 21st century should in some measure avoided in multi-generational worship. This is not to draw a firm line here, because most people understand "Thee, Thou, Thy" etc... and it's good to stay in touch with our heritage, so this does not altogether discount them. But they need to serve the focused purpose of worshipping with understanding. Many traditional strophic hymns seek to rhyme at all costs (whether or not the word makes logical sense). Others use absurd contractions to fit the melody. Of course, some hymns still work fine with older language, and sometimes a word can simply be taught afresh to the next generation, so that they sing intelligently. (Cultural wisdom will determine if this is a useful exercise or not for a given song/reading.)

Music is the language of culture; poetry the language of experience. Therefore, our worship ought to reflect the thoughts, words and experiences of today's worshippers. In the context of biblical truth, we seek to speak people's heart language. In some churches there is a deplorable absence of the "new song." If there are no fresh expressions of worship to engage the mind, soul, body and spirit, we will fall into worship "ruts" where vain repetition replaces heartfelt expression. New songs show corporate vitality and are a mark of health for your church. This is not suggesting that the old be thrown out simply because it is old, and we've already discussed this.

You probably should not lead more than one new song per Sunday, and repeating a new song for three consecutive weeks will help it stick in the corporate repertoire better. It's helpful to remember that musicians will learn and tire of music faster than the general congregation. Some in the church will not even recognize a song after you've sung in a half dozen times. Over a six-month period you'll need to keep coming back to those new songs to ensure they stick. Of course you may discover that a new song, for whatever reason, is not working. Give it about eight tries in six months. That is about the threshold of when people will truly "own" a song or not. And, while you're at it, remember most congregations will struggle to learn even 12-15 new songs a year. It is sometimes wise to chart out the top dozen songs you want to teach in a year. That way you can regulate the introduction of new songs. Keep a spreadsheet on what dates songs have been done. If you're like me, you might actually find this stat keeping enjoyable, but then again, I'm a nerd. If not enjoyable, keeping track is still very practical and will help you with your CCLI copy report as well. (If you don't know what CCLI is, check out www.ccli.com. Every church using modern worship music requires a license to do so.)

This next item is not so technical, but a must as you lead and teach and implement worship renewal. The more *mature* disciples in a church need to come to terms that their role in the church should be changing as they mature. (i.e. An interest more in making disciples than one's own personal preferences for a given style of music.) This does not mean throwing out all the old songs, but rather making *plenty* of room for the new, and encouraging the older generation to place a high value on passing on the faith, ahead of their music.

Often a church will have a number of young musicians coming up who only understand today's music. While it doesn't hurt to culture them a little, we must avoid stifling these people by forcing them into playing a style of music that they simply don't resonate with. Likewise it is ridiculous to expect a 70-year old organist to learn to "groove" with the latest worship tunes. Each artist should serve God genuinely and bring the best offering that they are able to. You have to first own an offering before you can truly bring it to God. If it's not authentic, it's not an offering. But part of the true corporate experience is learning to appreciate other forms of worship from our own preference. This is grace and maturity at work, and is for both old and young to learn.

How to pick music: Music intended to be sung by the congregation must be made singable for the average person. So:

Melodies should be written in popular (common) rhythms avoiding difficult syncopation as much as possible. So things like eclectic rap, fusion, bluegrass, blues etc… may be on the fringe UNLESS that is the dominant makeup of your congregation, in which case you should be doing these styles. Melodies should be in a singable range, approx. A-D. There will have to be discretion exercised to determine how much higher than 'D' we can go before we start to lose people. For example a passage that dabbles with E flat or even E may be fine, so long as it is only a bar or two, or perhaps at a climactic key change finale. If you have a boisterous, singing congregation, you'll be able to sing all the Matt Redman, Hillsong and Chris Tomlin songs in their original keys. If you're a normal person like me, you have to bring everything done by these artists down, sometimes several keys!

The CCLI top 100 is a great way to gauge the accessibility and broad appeal of songs. The CCLI top 100 is very valuable, as it measures for the global church some of the most singable, memorable and meaningful worship songs that resonate over the whole earth, not just your country. There is something of high value in making sure your church knows at least 25% of these songs. There seems to be a real theme of God-anointed worship in them, when you consider how God is moving over the whole earth. So think about keeping your music catalogue inclusive of, A) a fairly high percentage of internationally popular songs B) some national, C) some regional, and even some D) from your own musicians.

Accompaniment should *accompany*, not constantly overpower the vocals. In other words, if the words can't be heard, you need to pull back the instruments or boost the vocals. Similarly, if the music does at some point become louder than the volume of the congregation (and this may be ok) it should be only momentary, giving way to the congregation's voices being heard. We always want to be able to hear the vocals - even in worship environments that are very loud.

There should be an artistic unity that integrates logic in the marriage of music to lyrics. So, reflective passages should have sensitive accompaniment. Words of jubilant praise should be full of energy. There are some hymns (that shall remain nameless to protect the guilty) that have wonderful, deep lyrics set to the most cheese-ball music on the planet. *I was sinking deep in sin, far from the peaceful shore...* (Oops, I guess I couldn't keep that one anonymous after all.)

Dynamics in music communicate emotion. Many worship bands play everything at the same volume and same intensity, not allowing music to breathe or be felt, creating this aggravating "wall of noise". (Did I hear an Amen?!) One of my pastors referred to this kind of worship as "thrash and bash." I like it loud, but skill has to enter the picture somewhere! Some drummers only have two volumes: much too loud, and still much too loud. Music is supposed to say something through expressiveness, not just provide white noise for the text of a song. By the way, I love my drummers, and I am one myself.

A word on drama

Drama can be a powerful communication tool. But it may also cause a conflict with worship because it is so spectator oriented. In many situations I've been in, it seemed better to save dramas for bigger productions so that the participatory nature of worship is not lost. But there are some amazing worshipful dramas out there, that just cry for response. So if you discern that they are helpful, here are some suggestions.

- They need to portray Bible scenes or biblical principles being worked out in real life. The further you move from the biblical narrative, the further you've likely moved into performance that lacks context.
- The final product usually should facilitate response, i.e. clearly set up a transition to a form of worship response or sermon.
- Dramas should cause observers to easily identify with one or more characters with an emphasis on personal application.

- Again, the danger in drama is that it can quickly reduce the congregation to being spectators. Though drama can be very powerful, it is really suited toward the teaching/preaching ministry primarily. So think about using it as a bridge from the devotional worship experience to the message rather than using your worship time for drama.

A word on dance

- Care needs to be taken to ensure that attire is *overly* modest and that moves are in no way provocative.
- Dance, like drama, should engage people while telling a biblically pointed story.
- Dance needs to facilitate response in our hearts rather than only observation.
- In some church situations dance might only be deemed appropriate as a worshippers response in the congregation rather than an up-front display. (i.e. more a personal expression during corporate worship than a presentation on stage)

A word on prophecy/ sharing/ spontaneity

A special spontaneous word from worshippers can make for a great worship time. Often sentence prayers of adoration or thanksgiving are very meaningful, as they encourage ownership. Similarly, the reading of Psalms or other Scriptures out loud from within the body can be powerful in creating an atmosphere of worship.

If your church is open to the Spirit's work through prophecy, it may still be desirable for words from within the flock to be cleared with the Elders before a service. This can save a lot of damage control later. However, Elders should lead out as they feel prompted by the Holy Spirit with a message from God. If the Spirit gives an utterance to an Elder, they should feel free to speak or pray any time there is a sensitive moment in worship that they discern it is appropriate to speak into the body and further lead people toward the heart of God. That is to say that the entire leadership of a church ought to be the lead worshippers. As such we will gladly break away from the program if we feel the Spirit's leading. Any prophesy must clearly line up with Scripture and be useful to the body as a whole. Any special word should not put attention on the one speaking but rather keep attention on God and His glorious truth.

In corporate sharing there is sometimes a tension in testimonies that begin to focus too much on details of the story or the speaker. It is therefore best in a corporate setting to be brief on details and more focused on articulating the goodness of God. The congregation will probably be in a perpetual state of learning to keep the focus on God's character rather than their personal details. The teaching and example of the spiritual leadership will be helpful in upholding this expectation. Sometimes pre-recording testimonies is best. That way you can edit and really get at the main focus.

Banners are typically most effective as they contain the names and attributes of God and Scripture. The idea is that it is God's name that goes before us in worship, as it is a spiritual battle, and He is the Victor and our focus. Banners paraded can create an atmosphere of majesty appropriate for worship.

Other physical expressions of worship: (reclaiming tolerance)

A spirit of mutual tolerance, unity and Christian charity ought to be our atmosphere in corporate worship. We have so often been conditioned in the western political world to believe that tolerance means "accept as the same," when it technically means "accept as different." When we stop enforcing our *opinions* on others we discover true freedom in our church and in worship. Did we forget that Jesus came to relieve us from the burden of the law, and instead gave us the law of grace? How many times do churches make rules on how people dress, what entertainment they are to use, what qualifications they have to meet before they are "in?" Let's stop this foolishness for the sake of what actually matters...

While worshipping corporately, we need to be careful not to be an obnoxious distraction to others. On the other hand, just because you don't particularly enjoy or utilize a particular biblical form of worship does not give you permission to squelch others who want to. Both concepts of spontaneity and order need to be held in balance as directed by the spiritual leadership of a given church.

Often, especially in conservative circles, it is the spiritual leadership of the church that must provide teaching and direction for the introduction of the elements of worship that might be seen as a departure from the norms of a particular congregation/denomination. As the spiritual leaders teach, they should also begin to demonstrate the various forms of worship. This will be perceived as the blessing and consent, and it will have the desired ripple effect on the congregation as all begin to enjoy biblical freedom in worship expression.

Conclusion

We love happy endings, and even though there is plenty of heartache and disappointment as we lead the flock, we should celebrate and thank God every time even one person "gets it" and finally experiences surrender in worship. In ministry we live to see lives transformed. It keeps us going and encourages us. Two verses always come back to me, and as I close I hope you will be encouraged with them. I Corinthians 15:58 - that gem for those who serve in God's church: *We know that our labor in the Lord is not in vain.* The second one that constantly hits the "reset" button on all that I do, John 15:5 – Jesus couldn't be more direct: *Apart from Me you can do nothing.* Let's remember that at the end of the day, our people's response to God is a Holy Spirit thing. We can put all the right information and focus in place for worship to happen, but it is God at work in people's lives that brings the increase.

Nonetheless, we live in perilous times. Times when the "itching ears" are being catered to at the expense of the truth that delivers souls from hell. Brothers and sisters, I would plead with you: For the Renown of His Name, let's put Christ back at the center of Worship. To Him be all the glory in the church forever, Amen.

The story of God is still being written. Our experience of worship, as great as it may be, is only in part. I don't want to finish this book on a note of finality, because I have not arrived. I don't have all the answers and don't have the monopoly on truth in worship. (Though I've learned some pretty cool tricks along the way!) It is with that studious perspective that I hope you have enjoyed reading this book, and will continue to pursue our Holy God and ever seek to *make His praise glorious* in the church!